ymire

Dedication

This book is dedicated to God, our Heavenly Father who Spoke and life began; to all who confess, profess, proclaim and declare the Word of God as Truth and thereby impart life;

Acknowledgements

I acknowledge the Lordship of Jesus Christ, my personal Savior and Lord.

Thank you to the editors and staff at Xulon Press. The words herein as well as any errors or omission are the sole responsibility of this author.

I acknowledge Dr. Cora Benson, the high school English teacher who taught us how to speak; Professor Eleanor Paulson who taught us the beauty of articulate speech; Professor Jane Blankenship who taught us the potential of the spoken word. Thank you to Dr. Carol Parks Bani, my dear, dear friend and confidante and encour-

ager; to Ms. Stella Moody whose steadfast friend-
ship and encouragement to keep writing motivated
me beyond my own limitations (Thank God for the
The Master's Bookstore –and the best cup of tea
and fellowship – it's so warm, it's a wonder we ever
leave); to Pastor Clara Coleman, my dear friend
and sister colleague in the Gospel and true inter-
cessor, thank you for all of your prayers and love
and faithfulness; to Mrs. Evangeline Hankinson,
my friend and "mother" in the Lord; to Dr. Alice
Brown Collins, my friend, accountability/writing/
prayer partner-Thank God for our O. G. times;

I honor and appreciate both my Dad and
Mother and their legacy of commitment to Christ;
to my beautiful sisters Mrs. Janice Davis and
Mrs. Faye Chambers and their families. And, in
more ways than I can articulate, this book is a
tribute to my Mother, Mrs. Beatrice Criss, who

modeled Godly womanhood and taught us what it meant to be "daughters of destiny"; My deepest gratitude for her prayers, love, keen discernment and believing in her children and for consistently speaking the truth in love during her lifetime.

Thank you to the Saints of the Church of God in Christ and for the deeply held tradition of sermonic excellence and respect for the Spoken Word; for speaking destiny to us. Thank you to Reverends Harold and Marilyn Lambe and your family for modeling integrity and excellence; and challenging and helping us to walk through the open doors. Thank you to Madam Florence Yeboah, "Our Mother", and the women of Ghana who exemplify such great faith and dignity. A heartfelt thank you to my beloved Church family...New Covenant Church International and the extended New Covenant Church family in the

U.S.A. and in Ghana and beyond...Thank you for

your prayers, your support and your love. *Special*

thank you to my dear family...my beloved hus-

band, Bishop Joseph Quainoo whose authoritative

voice is unmistakable even as he is a passionate

minister of the Gospel of Jesus Christ – Thank

you Dear for your encouragement and support in

helping me to complete this task. Thank you for

your wisdom and for consistently speaking life to

us and helping us to walk by faith and not by sight.

Thank you to our precious sons-Timothy, Matthew

and John, young men of God's Grace and Favor,

soldiers and destiny keepers. You are my inspira-

tion and great delight! Be strong, Be courageous.

Walk in sterling faith and always, always, abso-

lutely always obey God and say what God says.

*Speak Truth to the people....**SPEAK LIFE!***

TABLE OF CONTENTS

SPEAK LIFE

THE BLESSING OF SPEAKING TO BLESS OTHERS

Wisdom is found on the lips of him who has

understanding (Proverbs 10:13)

INTRODUCTION

Speak...Parlez, Hablar, Kasa... In every language, the act of speaking is the wonderful, powerful faculty God has given to human beings for the purpose of communicating. Although we can communicate in ways other than using the human voice, it is the spoken word which enables us to communicate at some of the highest levels of meaning. "The fact that speakers are perceived as powerless or powerful based on the way that they talk means that language can be an important tool..." (Hackman, 2000). Consider the seeming innocence of a single spoken word. One word spoken, no consequences, no impact, no effect, right? Let's look closer. The Bible says the power of life and death are in the tongue. A word can potentially kill or bring life to a person. Yes, a single word is powerful. When that one word is spoken the right way in the right context – that power can be unleashed and bring about tremendous results for the good, ultimately for the Glory of God. This book is about what it means to intentionally harness the power of the spoken word for the good; as an act of blessing.

In essence, how can we bless one another with our words? Can we really impact a person for the good just by speaking? What if we spoke only those things which encourage, cleanse, heal and lift up. Nothing negative. Nothing doubtful. Not in fear. Not in resentment...Even in confrontation or expressing difficult truths and troubling emotions, we can still have as our underlying motive, the purpose of blessing. What if we made a conscious decision to allow the Holy Spirit to be in charge of our speech? We would say what God wants us to say. We would "speak life". As you read the following pages, may you think carefully about the purpose of the spoken word; about the marvelous faculty of speech and God's original intent for us to use our tongue to uplift, bear one another's burdens and truly love each other. In St John chapter 17, Jesus teaches His disciples in a passionate explanation about the Father's great love and His desire to see us love one another even as the Father and Son love one another:

> *"But now I come to You and <u>these things I</u> <u>speak</u>...that they all may be one as You, Father are in Me and I in You; that they also may be one in Us that the world may believe that You sent Me...that they may be one just as We are one. (St John 17:13, 21, 22).*

When we speak life to each other, we love one another even as God, our Father and Jesus, His Beloved Son love one another. We mirror that great love to the world. Even the world cannot deny the uniqueness and beauty of ardent, honest realness between believers. This is the kind of lifestyle that attracts unbelievers and through the power of the Holy Spirit wins them to faith in Christ. This is truly irresistible love. May God's grace anoint you to receive as you read. May these words help you to choose your words in accordance to God's Word and make you a blessing as you speak life.

CHAPTER ONE

Reconciling, Re-claiming, Redeeming...When Speaking Heals

Now all things are of God who has reconciled us

to Himself through Jesus Christ and has given us

the ministry of reconciliation (II Corinthians 5:18)

H ow does speaking life change my own life and impact the lives of others around me? One purpose for speech is to heal and redeem broken and damaged hearts. Knowing our propensity for emotional pain, God designed us with the ability to speak in His Name and minister healing and redemption to one another. The ultimate healing begins and ends with addressing and resolving our broken relationship with the Father, God Almighty. The Apostle Paul calls this the ministry of reconciliation, being restored in our hearts to God and humans. This can play out in intense, complex relationships or in every day interactions. Wherever broken relationships are intercepted and reconnected in God's love and grace, it is, in part, the result of speaking life. Most often, someone took the time to speak into the situation and call those involved into reconciliation. For a moment, consider this encounter between brothers.

"You always bother me!"

"You bother me more!!"

"You're a big baby"

"You're a big baby too!"

"No, you're the one who's always crying"

"I am not!"

"You 're crying now"

"I am not"

With the last shout came an explosion of tears as my youngest son melted in a dramatic heap of frustration and defeat. Typically, I do not enter into my sons' daily squabbles. I've encouraged them to understand that conflict is a normal part of life and that they can work through their differences and remain close as brothers. This outburst seemed a little different and begged intervention. With deliberate steps, I entered the boys' bedroom and began to speak to them. Without a long lecture, I challenged them to reverse the content of their last exchange. I explained that I was not going to stop them from arguing but every time I heard them argue, I was going to insist they speak to one another nicely – to the same extent that they spoke to one another harshly. And that I reserved the right to "approve" their choice of words.

My sons quickly learned that a certain level of aggression during conflict rendered a consequence of having to speak the opposite- equal to the measure of their aggressive language. For instance, if in their anger or upset they spoke and said "I don't even like you". The corresponding redress of that statement might be "Not only do I like you, I also appreciate you very much!" If the offense was particularly wounding, I would make them add, "I love you my brother, whom I love dearly". They would rather say or do almost anything other than saying those words. It was absolutely tortuous. With grimaced faces, they would force the words. At other times, they would laugh and tease to distract from the sheer discomfort of being so "sappy". But gradually they learned that their words have consequences.

WHEN SPEAKING IS NOT BLESSING

There are many words that are spoken which do not bring blessing but to the contrary, these kinds of words invite negativity, trouble, hurt, even death. There are many forms of "hostile" words. When we allow ourselves to speak these words, we are making a choice and the end result is not blessing. Most often, we are tearing down or breaking trust which is foundational to all successful relationships.

Various Capacities of Words

Often, we adopt word types and patterns of speaking from others around us. As children, we learn from our parents what to say and how to say it. Families take on what I call "a speaking direction". They tend to be prone to speaking up or speaking down. Think for a moment about how you identify people to their families. We might say, "he looks just like his Daddy". Have you ever thought that "he sounds just like his Daddy". We inculcate accent, hand gestures, posture and a spiritual bend in our speaking personality from our parents and family upbringing. Some families speak loudly, shouting out their ideas and feelings at one another. Other families speak barely above a whisper. Although there might be many people in the house, the atmosphere is quiet and pensive. Still others internalize rituals of hate and destructive emotions consequently speaking in cynical, strident and downcast ways. They might laugh and justify their cruel tongue as "just kidding around". They might even say home is the place where "I can be myself" and speak in unguarded ways.

Really, what is taking place is an establishing of a way of talking along with a way of thinking which results in either life-giving or life-destroying utterances and actions. What follows is a closer look at various functions of words which can be life-giving (blessing) or life-destroying (cursing). Let's consider the negative ones first and contemplate what speaking life is not and then consider what speaking life is.

Characteristics of Words That Function Negatively

Hostile

Hurtful

Hindering

Hiding

Hardening

Hoaxing

Hyping

Characteristics Of Words That Are Used To Bless

Helpful

Hospitable (Hosting)

Honoring

Hopeful

Honest

Humorous

Holistically

Holy

As we speak, we must evaluate the effect and impact the words are having on our own lives and on others. Are we leaving a negative effect around us? Or, do the words we speak have a positive, encouraging and uplifting aura, leaving others feeling impacted for the good; feeling blessed? I have been in situations where friends or significant people in my life have confronted me with what might be considered 'a hard word' but after the confrontation, because of the careful and caring words that were chosen, I've walked away feeling hopeful and with dignity and self-respect in place. This is because the person spoke firmly and told me not so much what I wanted to hear but what I needed to hear. I recognize that there are times when even the most carefully chosen words are still displeasing and offensive to the person who is being confronted. If that person is sincere about wanting God's will they will come around later to agree that for the moment, the words were hard but in the long term, the confrontation was good for them.

Oh, The Tongue - A Little Member, A Lot Of Potential For Impact

The Word of God says the tongue is "a little member that boasts great things" James 3:5). In fact, the potential and function of the tongue is compared to that of a rudder on a ship. "Look also at ships: although they are so large and driven by fierce winds, they are turned by a very small rudder wherever the pilot desires" (James 3:4). The tongue is a euphemism, a reference which stands for the mouth, the capability of speech as well as the actual words spoken. This capacity to speak cannot be contained by human strength alone. "No man can tame the tongue. It is an unruly evil" (James 3:8). An implicit consequence is in verse 5. "See how great a forest a little fire kindles! And the tongue is a fire..." (James 3:5). Let's look closer at the context of James chapter 3. First, chapter 3 follows the hallmark teaching about faith and works. (For as the body without the spirit is dead, so faith without works is dead also. James 2;26). Chapter 3 opens with a warning against casually becoming a teacher; teaching without being aware of this fundamental truth, that the teacher "shall receive a stricter judgment". The admonition comes with the warning that if anyone does not stumble in word, he is perfect, able to bridle the whole body. Another implicit connection is drawn here, that not stumbling in word (talking too much, or talking wrongly) is likened to being perfect and "perfect" is likened to discipline. It is the state of discipline which is comparable to the bridling of a horse. The person who disciplines his words is able to discipline his whole body.

From this introduction, James focuses on the fundamental role of speech (the tongue) with six comparisons; the bit in the horse's mouth, the rudder of the ship, fire, deadly poison, fresh water and bitter (salt) water. Each comparison illustrates the potential of the spoken word to bless or curse. As believers, Christ wants us to be conscious of this potential and choose blessing. The instruction is straightforward, "Out of the same mouth proceed blessing and cursing. My brethren, these things ought not to be so." (James 3:10).

With our tongue we can have tremendous impact on the lives of others around us. We can create trouble, hurt and confusion by dropping innuendos or negative suggestions or full-blown accusations. Even if certain information is factual, we should still prayerfully think and consider the consequences before sharing it. There are some other guidelines which should govern our sharing of information. Consider the following questions as just a few ways to evaluate why, when and how you speak:

*What is the motive of your sharing?

*Are you sharing the information to cause hurt?

*Are you sharing the information to get revenge?

*Is your sharing unwise?

*Is it untimely?

*Is there any sense of power or control in your speaking?

*Are you sure the information is indeed the truth?

*Have you considered that there might be more information unknown to   you. The unknown information might change the overall understanding of the matter?

For we know in part and see in part, the Lord sees the whole. Let's make sure that we are speaking truthfully and in earnest.

SAYING WHAT GOD SAYS

As we consider our words, we can ask ourselves what is our speaking direction - more

importantly who are we imitating and who do
we sound like when we speak? When we become
Christians we become new in Christ. We become
"new creations" in Christ. Old things are passed
away and all things have become new". Part of the
'all things' includes our speech and the way we
communicate with others. On one level, we will
still bear the physical resemblances of our parents and earthly family, but our spiritual nature
is changed. Consequently we are changed from
the inside out and everything in our nature that
is destructive, unclean and negative is now by
faith cleansed out of us. When I was growing up,
some of the older people in our Church used to
say it this way, "I got a new walk. I got a new
talk...". The Holy Spirit who comes to reside in
us begins to convict us of evil doing and coarse
ways of dealing with others; this includes rough

talking, foolish joking, crude speech, condemning criticism and all manner of hateful words. So, we take on the speaking direction of our Heavenly Father. No matter what speaking direction our families have had, God changes us so that we take on His nature and this is definitely manifested in our speech.

Saying what God says encompasses speaking what He wants us to say and saying it the way He would have us to say it. The question again, *how can we bless one another with our words?* What does it take to live a lifestyle of encouragement, intentionally using our words to uplift, inspire, motivate and strengthen one another in Christian love? Scripture teaches us the importance of stirring one another to good works. Surely, this means we are to use our words as a way of stirring and inciting our brothers and sisters to progress – to move forward in their devotion and

service to one another and ultimately, to God.

We are to live out our mandate to serve rather

than be served and to give which is even more

of a blessing than receiving. This means pointing

others to Christ. In effect, we do not have to wait

for the "right" moment to say words that bless the

spirit; to quote Scripture; to paraphrase Scripture

or mention the Goodness of the Lord. Often, just

mentioning the Name of the Lord in sincerity can

bless the hearer and encourage him/her in pow-

erful ways. There are two specific ways we can

accomplish speaking blessing - speak to a person

encouraging words about him/her and speak to a

person encouraging words about the Lord. For a

moment, let's look closer at these approaches to

blessing one another.

Yes, words are the mechanism by which we fulfill a part of our obligation to each other. Words are powerful, moreover speaking words – vocalizing, writing, signing or artistically representing them has the great potential of blessing. When we bless one another, we fulfill the command of Jesus to love one another. We are to love our neighbor as we love ourselves. While this means being responsible in many ways (such as helping our neighbor shovel snow or tend the lawn), speaking affirming words to them is certainly what Jesus had in mind. But often we fall short. Have you ever walked away from a conversation feeling that you did not say what you really wanted to say. Perhaps, you said many things you did not want to say. Still, such experiences leave us feeling empty and wondering "why didn't I think of that while I was with him/her?"

For some, the struggle is between knowing how one feels but not knowing how, when or if to express it. Or, we may be confused or concerned about how our words will or will not be received. There are so many potential roadblocks to successful communication. In a simple exchange between two people, there are several layers of interpretations going on; what I feel, what I think you feel, what I want to say, what I think you might say in reaction to what I said, how you feel, how you think I feel, what you want to say and what you think I might say in reaction to what you said. Then there is the actual message spoken and my own reaction to what I said...*I didn't mean to say it like that* – Your actual spoken reaction to what I said and your thoughts about what you said...*I wonder if she understands a word I just said.* Confused, anyone?!

And, then there are cases where there is confusion or misunderstanding at the content level.
Please consider the following example from one
of my student's papers. I asked the class to prepare a one-page story sharing one of "Life's Most
Embarrassing Moments". To preserve confidenti-
ality I will not reveal her identity but her story is
called "Club Sandwich".

*"As a summer job, I work as a cart girl at a local
golf course. My job is to serve drinks and assist
the golfers as much as possible with anything they
need. It's a great job and a lot of fun...It was one
of my first days at work...It was toward the end of
the day and a golfer stopped to ask me a favor. He
asked me to retrieve his sandwich out of the office
in the clubhouse. Of course, I couldn't say no, even
though it was a bit of a pain to drive all the way*

back to the clubhouse, but I did it anyway. Upon getting there I realized the office was locked. I asked everyone working in the office to help me to unlock the door and help look for this man's sandwich. We turned the office upside down and did not find any sandwich at all.

Reluctantly, I drove all the way back to the golfer to inform him that there was no sandwich in sight. He started to become a little annoyed and repeatedly stated, "no, a sand-wich. It's a CLUB!". *So equally annoyed, I drove all the way back to the clubhouse and begged the rest of the co-workers to help me look for the man's now 'club sandwich'. Once again, no luck at all and I was forced to return to this man with nothing but a word from my boss who drove back with me to inform the golfer personally that there was no club sandwich.*

It turns out that the man was never asking for a sandwich or a club sandwich for that matter. Instead, he was asking me to get his "sand wedge" as he pointed to one of his golfing clubs. I was so embarrassed. What a miscommunication!

(From the University of Rhode Island Communication Studies Project, January, 2011)

Often, the problem is a miscommunication or misunderstanding of words or both. It is important to take the time to listen to others as they speak and remember it is helpful to ask for clarification.

In some cases, we become embroiled in conflict and relational strife and then put up the defenses by making excuses or changing the subject. All of us have different strategies for dismissing or deflecting what we don't want to hear or talk about. For me, avoiding conflict often becomes paramount to working through the conflict and reaching resolution. Sometimes the thought of the conflict is so unsettling, frightening or too emotionally threatening that I convince myself that I will address it later and then lapse into a kind of unhealthy co-existence with the problem, often tucking the problem away at the subconscious level. Again, this is not healthy. From experience over the years, I have learned that the problem never really goes away. We must engage and this means trusting God for the courage, strength and honesty to face the issue. It also means seeking Him for wisdom, timing and guidance in facing the truth. With God's wisdom come the *words* to speak to the situation and to the persons involved in the situation.

There is yet another issue that can hinder the speaking of kind words to one another. Let's consider again the words of Jesus. Love your neighbor as yourself. How can we love our neighbor when we don't love ourselves? Perhaps a big part of the problem is that we have not settled the issue of loving ourselves and receiving our own giftedness, uniqueness and purpose in Christ. After all, how is it that I can be the object of God's love...?!

In the brokenness of our humanity we often settle for much less than Christ has for us. We live so beneath our privilege as His disciples. We deprive ourselves of the joy and bliss of Christian living which is living as one who is reconciled to God. One comparison that comes to mind is the difference between driving a car that is poorly aligned and one that is aligned properly. To live with "unaddressed" baggage is to live constantly skewed off course of who we are meant to be individually and corporately (This idea of corporate reconciliation is developed further in chapter five on *Speaking Life – Building Community*). To live as one who is reconciled is to live in the forward thrust of a smoothly navigated course. Although the course may be filled with challenges and emotional bumps and detours, we will have a secure sense of where we are going and who's ultimately driving. We must come to fully accept ourselves in light of this foundational truth - **God loves us and He sent His Son, Jesus Christ to die for our sins. Jesus' atoning death redeemed us from the eternal curse and penalty of sin, therefore we are free. We are redeemed. We are not guilty of our past. Our hope for eternal life and fulfilled life is secure in Jesus Christ!** Take a moment to reflect on this truth...For those of you reading this right now and you realize that you have never accepted Jesus Christ as your personal Savior, I invite you to pray this prayer right now, *Dear Jesus I recognize that I need You. I acknowledge that You are the Son of God and that You are the way to true spiritual life and freedom. I admit that just like every human being, I am a sinner, that is my nature. I need to be forgiven of my sins. Please forgive me. I accept that You are the only One who can save me from my sins. You died on the cross for me and your perfect, sinless Blood paid the price for my sins and for all of the sins of all people every where. Wash me of my sins. Cleanse me and come into my heart. Let Your Holy Spirit live inside of me and make me more and more like You. I give you my heart and I ask You to be my Lord. Thank you. Amen.* If you have just prayed this prayer and you were sincere in praying, you have now become a Christian! Jesus Christ is now your personal Lord and Savior and you have just begun a new, wonderful relationship with Him! I am excited for you and I have prayed for you. The next steps include, tell another Christian about your decision, attend a Bible-believing Christian Church in your area where you live and ask a Christian pastor or counselor for a Bible and a daily devotional guide. (*Our Daily Bread* is a suggested resource. *You may request one at www.rbc.org or Box 2222, Grand Rapids, MI 49501.* Begin praying and reading the Bible every day. Remember, your relationship with Jesus is now personal and praying and reading the Bible is a way of communicating with Jesus every day. Spend at least 10 to 15 minutes every day in a quiet place and pray. Begin by worshipping God, praise Him for His Goodness - how He created nature, your family, your own life. Thank Him for His love and His provision for you (He is the One who supplies your daily needs for food, shelter, work etc...). After praising and thanking Him, tell Him your needs and ask for His help and intervention. Thank Him again for hearing you and believe that He will respond to your prayer. Then, spend some time reading your Bible. If you don't know where to begin, read in the book of St. John or Romans in the New Testament of the Bible. You might also want to read from the Psalms in the Old Testament. Use your devotional guide to help you apply the truths of the Bible. You are on your way to a deeply fulfilling spiritual life in Jesus Christ.

PRAISE BREAK - LET THE WORDS OF MY MOUTH...

For those of us who have been walking in Christ for a while, we are free in Jesus Christ. So, let this be an invitation to you - go ahead and spend a few moments in Praise and minister life to yourself by forgiving yourself and accepting Christ's love for you...Say this out loud

I am redeemed by the Blood of Jesus

I am forgiven

I am made whole in Him

I am no longer the person of my old past

I am a new creation in Christ

Christ's love for me is abundant and complete

Hallelujah!

Do you realize that loving yourself is not preoc-

cupation with yourself. It is not self-indulgence,

self-willed determination or self-centeredness,

No! *Loving yourself is simply receiving God's love.*

When you love yourself, you come into agreement

with God - agreeing with God that you are who He

says you are. And, God says you are precious, the

apple of His Eye! God says you are loved. God says

this about all of us, that we once were sinners

in need of a Savior. Because of His great love for

us, God provided for our salvation and that is the

ultimate love. As stated earlier, the journey after

becoming a Christian, though filled with God's

love and the joy of knowing Him is not exempt

from daily testing and the challenges that come

along with living life but because of Christ, we are

newly aligned and we can be confident that we

will for all our struggles, arrive at our destination. Yes, we will! (This is a good time to say Amen!)

God wants our words, our daily talk to line up with these truths - that we are redeemed, we are now a part of a living, redemptive community, we are upward-focused, not downward-focused. He wants our words to reflect the power of His transformation in our lives. The words we speak should now bear the same mark as the words He speaks- life-giving, affirming, fresh, encouraging, insightful, restorative, building, creative....The old me is gone and the old ways of doing things including how I used to talk are gone. The old patterns of speech included defensiveness, arrogance, competitiveness, even profane and vulgar words. I didn't realize it but I was dying and my words were like bullets that cause death and tear and destroy. It wasn't a pretty sight.

One of the links between misery and continual negative talk is regret for the past. Often people feel utter helplessness in not being able to do anything about past mistakes and failures. It is like an awful prison. When asked about how they feel about their past, some said it was like being tied and bound to cruel reminders about "everything negative that had taken place in the past." This can be a tragic cycle. It is like the mistakes of the past cause punishing guilt which leads to negative talk about oneself and others. The negative talk acts like fertilizer to a garden, except instead of yielding flowers and beauty, it promotes more guilt and negativity which can lead to more mistakes and more sin. Once the cycle begins, the individual can feel "in so deep" that there is little hope for being rescued. The Apostle Paul captured this dilemma when he said, "who can deliver me from this body of death?"(Romans 7:24). This pro-

duces more negative words which causes more

spiritual death. What can break this cycle?

One of the many blessings of faith in Jesus

Christ is the breaking of this horrible cycle. The

Blood of Jesus breaks the spiritual bondage which

is a foundation and breeding ground for psycho-

logical bondage, emotional bondage which then

manifests destructively in the physical. Physical

abuse, whether it be physical violence against

another person or against oneself is rooted in

spiritual bondage. <u>We might even hide or mask</u>

<u>deep inner pain for long periods of time but tell-</u>

<u>tale signs are almost always found in the words of</u>

<u>the person who is hurting.</u> Verbal symptoms range

from verbal abusiveness to self-depreciation. Some

even use verbally intellectual sophistication. Such

words may even sound impressive but really the person is empty, tormented or in deep anguish.

This link between self-condemnation and negative speaking must be intercepted and broken through prayer and the Word of God. The person who needs this help must be willing to allow the Holy Spirit to teach him/her a whole new way of talking. Keep in mind that self-condemnation takes on many forms and can be present in people from all walks of life. At times, self-condemnation can become self-destruction without the person realizing what is happening. This can result in many types of seemingly harmless abusive behaviors that, left unchecked, gradually gain ground in the life of the person and eventually make the person's life out of control. Behaviors such as overeating, eating disorders (for example, anorexia and bulimia), alcohol abuse, drug abuse, sexual immorality and other forms of abuse are typically accompanied by negative confession. And, quite often negative behaviors can persist not only in the presence of negative confession but also where there is no positive confession. In other words, the person might not be a chronic verbal abuser and he might even seem like a very "nice" person but there is no confession of the Word of God in his mouth. There is no speaking about the truth of one's pain and the truth of God's provision to address that pain. It is a spiritual problem that requires a spiritual solution and in this context, no confession can be as debilitating as negative confession. This is because words are spiritual and have spiritual implications. The spiritual realm around us responds to exact, faith-filled purposeful words. None of this neutral stuff! Spiritual principalities and strongholds do not recognize passive, words that tout co-existence and spiritual tolerance and pseudo-peace. This might be difficult for us to grasp because many of us are counting on our "niceness", which is nothing more than bland timidity, to win us points with our adversary. Somehow, we fool ourselves in thinking that if I am just neutral and not offensive to anybody, any enemies that I might have will discount me as no threat and as we use to say "cut me some slack" or "let me off the hook". While other people in my camp are punished, somehow I will slide by.

This brings to mind the story of Esther in the Bible. God opened the door for her to find great favor with the King. For a season, she found it comfortable to live in silence about the condition of her people, the Jews. Her uncle Mordecai had to give her what we might call a reality check and remind her that after all, "Esther, you also are a Jew and if the persecution against Jews is fully expressed, you will be numbered as one of us." In other words, your silence is not going to prevent your destiny as a Jew. The only thing that will help is assertive, demonstrative and clear action. Mordecai helped Esther to understand that you are the one in the position to help and part of that help will have to be in the form of spoken words. You can't get around it. You can't just exist as neutral to this problem. You will have to declare a position or it will be declared for you. I can imagine Mordecai sounding like one of my uncles and saying to Esther, *Girl, you gonna have to go in there and talk to the King and you open up your mouth and speak like you know...and you can't be mushy-mouthed or talking around the point. You have to tell the King just how it is.* Mordecai continued with one of the most well-known obser-vations recorded in Scripture, "For who knows, Esther, that the Lord has brought you to the kingdom for such a time as this" (Esther 4:13-14).

Let me reiterate, the spiritual world does not recognize neutrality. If you don't declare who you are and what you stand for, the enemy will respond in several ways. Let me point out two of the ways that the enemy responds to the silent and/or passive Christian. First, the devil hates that you are a Christian and will fight you with discouragement. So, the enemy completely ignores your passivity. Your silence does not win any brownie points of goodness with the enemy. No persecution reduction for good behavior! In what we might call, Bible language, "woe" to the person who thinks he can buddy with the enemy and somehow escape the enemy's strikes and evil attacks. Let me point to an unfortunate incident that resulted in death. I apologize for using this example because it is absolutely horrendous, but I think it so clearly paints the picture of the vile purposes of the enemy and the danger of letting our guard down.

A man took for his personal pets, some wild lizards, several of them! They ranged in size from 2 feet or more. The largest one was more than 6 feet long. This man unwisely came to "love" the lizards, giving them full range of his two bedroom apartment. The lizards roamed the apartment unchecked, perching wherever and eating whenever and wherever he fed them. On more than one occasion, the lizards bit the man. One time they bit him on the arm so severely that he showed his co-workers the wound at his job. The men who worked with him, (he was a car salesman), tried to convince him that the lizards were becoming too big and too aggressive and that once they crossed the line of biting their master, they have exhibited an unhealthy disregard for their master's life. He ignored their warnings.

One day the man was late in coming to work. In fact, the whole day passed and he did not arrive at work at all and it was unlike him to miss work. The next day he was still absent and not answering his phone. Finally, his employer called the police. The police went to the man's apartment and forced entry to find the lizards walking about. That is not all they found. Without sensational-izing the gory details, the evidence pointed to the lizards. It appeared that they had killed the man and had begun to devour his body. (www.animal planet.com/fatal attractions)

This example is not to offend you and again I'm sorry because the example even made me feel squeamish at the sheer thought of such a terrible encounter but I believe this is how the enemy works in the lives of people who become too familiar and do not read and speak God's Word. We can be fooled into thinking that we can co-habit with the enemy. We can even become unaware that the enemy is indeed a real enemy and if given an opportunity will devour us. Thank God for His amazing Grace and protection. God will keep us but let us not be foolish and care-less and think that our unwillingness to fight by speaking God's Word will make the enemy less intent on destroying us.

The personal level of attack effects the indi-vidual peace of mind and well-being. The enemy always wants to disturb us individually and make us personally upset, burdened and in turmoil. Sometimes, it can feel like the carrying of a heavy load on one's back or in the middle of one's chest. It can slow our responsiveness to our environment around us and make us function in a depressed state or even render us unable to function. This inability to function leads us to an understanding of the second area of attack-becoming ineffective as a minister/an ambassador of Jesus Christ and thereby unable to help, heal and strengthen others. *The Christian who is not active in speaking God's Word is a particular target for the enemy's attacks against the Church.* Your speaking the Word of God is a weapon to be used in spiritual warfare over your own life, but even more importantly, God wants each believer to be ready and useful for ministry. My readiness includes speaking the Word of God which will defend and protect the investment that God has placed not only in my life but in your life also. My ministry is for you and your ministry is for me. We are co-laborers in the Kingdom and speaking the Word of God is paramount in Kingdom life. My unwillingness to speak is a negation of the power of God that should flow unhampered throughout the Body of Christ.

Speaking Life Means Speaking Words That Validate One's Identity & Purpose As A Christian

One of the "privileges" of living as a Christian is making peace with our past, embracing ourselves and accepting our own existence as a validated affirmed, purposeful plan of God. Loving me takes on a whole new dimension. It is not about loving myself because I'm sufficient within myself. It is about loving and accepting the "me" that God loves and finds so worthy of His attention that He sent His Son, Jesus Christ to die for. If God can love me with all of my limitations, surely I can love me, accept me, forgive me...

What is a prime characteristic that accompanies this kind of freedom and acceptance? A positive inner conversation. Intrapersonally, we have an ongoing barrage of words daily. How much of this inevitable inner speaking is actually positive? Sometimes, we are not even aware that we are speaking negative words to ourselves on a regular basis. Throughout the day our self-talk is often filled with fearful, doubtful and sometimes condemning words. We so readily concentrate on those things which Christ cast into the sea of forgetfulness, nailed on the cross and separated from us and Himself as far as the east is from the west. Why are we so compelled to go excavate what the Lord has buried and forgotten? Could it be that we are so connected to our past because of deep powerful longings to re-write the past? Out of regret, shame or guilt we sometimes fixate on our moments of past failures, losses or private pain. We are quick to rehearse poor decisions, even good plans gone awry beyond our control. I do not mean to suggest that careful introspection and even retrospection is not useful. It is even required in order for us to grow and move on. I do mean to suggest that the beginning of blessing others is healthily blessing ourselves. It is a conscious decision to bless ourselves and *speak life over our own lives. Sometimes, you simply have to shake yourself and talk to yourself and speak the Word of God to you!* This is not haughty-minded self-exaltation but a re-defining of who we are in

light of who God says we are. Remember speaking

life is saying what God says, agreeing with Him

and letting His life-giving Words take the place

of our own words which often come short of the

potential for which they were created – to speak

life over our own lives; to impact others and bless

them. This means calling ourselves what God

calls us and coming into agreement with the Lord

and His proclamation over our lives.

In the next few moments, take time to list sev-

eral characteristics about yourself that bless you

when you think of them. Think about how God

has used you in the last few weeks, months or

even years. Realizing that it is not you, but the

power of God at work in you, take time to thank

God for changing you and maturing you into a

purposeful and effective Christian. Ask the Lord

to strengthen areas that need to be strengthened and make a fresh commitment to speak life over your own life. Perhaps you are reading this and you really don't know what to say to bless yourself. Maybe you might even be a really strong advocate for others who are defenseless, oppressed or in need of your guidance. But you realize that you really haven't taken much time to strengthen your own inner life. Subtly, you have become "down" on yourself and quite negative in your thinking about yourself. Please take a moment to pray this prayer and re-dedicate yourself to a positive, life-affirming thought life.

Holy Spirit cleanse me from the inside. I confess my need for your help. I make a conscious effort to stop all negative thoughts about myself which so easily become negative confessions and spoken utterances. Such words are detrimental to my spiritual and ultimately my physical well-being and so I ask you Holy Spirit to replace my negative talk with the Word of God. Help me to say what God says about me. Help me to confess the truth of Scripture and to talk with an upward, not a downward focus. I am redeemed. I am whole in Christ. I am healed in Christ. I am wealthy, having all of my needs met according to His riches and He enables me to be a giver and to help meet the needs of others. I acknowledge the Lord in all my ways and He directs my path. As I wait on Him, He renews my strength. I am safe in the Lord's perfect design and will for my life. He gives me the wisdom I need. He gives me the power to live free from sin. And He fills me with His joy. He will help me in my relationships, my work and in meeting my daily needs. My life matters and Jesus Christ is the fulfillment of my life. Thank you, Jesus. Amen.

Feel free to say this prayer daily, several times a day if you are so prompted. In fact, it is a good idea to write this prayer (or your own prayer) on an index card and post it on your dressing mirror, your refrigerator, place it in your brief case or book bag – whatever it takes to begin speaking the truth of God's Word about you, to you! Get ready, for this can be a revolutionary way of talking and living. Let's examine closer some of what the Lord says to us about us. There seems to be at least three areas in which the Lord speaks to us directly on this matter.

First, Jesus says, "Speak those things which are not as though they were"

Second, Scripture teaches us not to dwell on the sins of our past, *"For it is shameful even to speak of those things which are done by them in secret" (Ephesians 5:12).* While confession is good for the soul, be careful not to allow the sharing of past sins to become the preoccupation of your communication. For example, I recall how my husband and I watched a nationally televised "confession" of a well-known Minister who revealed how he had lived a double life as a cocaine addict. At first, his testimony seemed compelling. Quickly we both became uneasy as the Minister continued on for minutes rehearsing in great detail how he used to get high and the sensuous effects of the high and how he became quite adept at disguising his high and deceiving others. We became alarmed because he seemed to be giving too much time to the details and we did not hear him clearly state that he was now free from this addiction. Without judging this Minister, we were reminded that it is critical to "speak your life forward". Speak from your point of salvation, yes, but, let your speech and your confession point toward your destiny, your future in Christ. Again Ephesians 5 says, *"For you were once darkness, but <u>now you are light in the Lord. Walk as children of light."</u> (Verse 8)*. If we are not careful, we can get caught up in rehearsing explicit details of past sins. While, I recognize that some deliverance takes time and that many need to work through the pain of past hurts and sins, I believe that much of the healing comes from focusing on the Healer not just the wound. Still, some might have the question what if I am a Christian and I have prayed for deliverance but I am still feeling bound by a sin or memory of a sin. Speak with your Pastor, Prayer group leader or mature Christian, someone who can handle the confession and lead you in a prayer of repentance and break the bondage and soul tie to the persons, things or habits associated with your sinful past. After praying, that Christian leader can also help you to bury that sin by praying a prayer of freedom for you in Christ. From that point on, when you speak of that sin or experience, you can speak victoriously and put more of the emphasis on your journey toward wholeness and your destiny of greatness in Christ. In our local Church, we welcome new believers to a workshop called "Freedom Encounter". The facilitator explains the Scriptural basis for claiming freedom in Christ and then leads each participant in a renouncing of past sins and connections with sinful lifestyles. To end the session, he/she will pronounce freedom upon them and speak into their lives the Word of

God and the glorious plan of God's design for their future. It is a beautiful ministry and highly effective. At the center of that ministry is speaking life. What a blessing it is to see the redemptive work of grace and to know that this grace is available to each one of us. Yesterday's stuff is gone, washed away in the Blood of Jesus. Today is a new day and tomorrow never looked brighter!

Third, do not refuse the Lord's instruction. The Lord speaks in various ways and when He speaks, He expects us to listen and obey. The Lord also has emotions and we can so easily grieve the Holy Spirit when we reject what Jesus is saying to us. The Scriptures say it this way, *"See that you do not refuse Him who speaks. For if they did not escape who refused Him who spoke on earth, much more shall we not escape if we turn away from Him who speaks from heaven." (Hebrews 12:25).* The

Lord wants us to recognize His voice and readily receive His Words. This builds our faith and intimacy with the Lord and pleases the Lord. Think of how you feel when you say to a person, 'I will pick you up at 7 o'clock.' At the appointed time, you are at his/her doorstep ringing the doorbell but there is no answer. You call the person on the phone. 'Where are you? I said I would pick you up at 7 o'clock." Stridently, the person responds, 'Oh, I wasn't sure if you would really come so I called a taxi'. How would you feel? A little mistrusted? We do this to the Lord quite often. We hear a prophetic Word or read a promise in the Word of God and sense the witness that the promise is for me, but in a short amount of time we can reason ourselves out of believing that promise and prepare an alternative, 'in case things don't work out'.

The Lord is saying do not refuse His Word. Speaking what God has spoken to us is an expression of faith, demonstrable faith. The Lord is saying it is alright to put His Word on the line. He will come through. He will not leave you on a tightrope all alone. We simply need to be sure that we have indeed heard from the Lord and then speak it!

Getting Rid Of Sticks and Stones...Words that Reconcile and Redeem

Consider a time when you felt wounded by the words someone spoke to you. I'm sure that after such an encounter, you could readily agree that words really cause significant harm. The Bible says a word can kill or cause irreparable damage however the Bible also states that words can be redemptive and lead to reconciliation.

While the use of harsh words can be like jabbing a person with sticks or like throwing stones, the use of kind words can be like the application of soothing balm. Such words are healing, redemptive and reconciling. One of the key areas where redemption and reconciliation occurs is in the act of forgiveness. Cultivating a forgiving heart and lifestyle is so important that Jesus teaches us to forgive one another and love not just in words but also in deed and action. While they are important, actions should not dismiss or diminish the importance of using forgiving and restoring words. Often, asking to be forgiven and subsequently granting forgiveness is the action that is urgently needed for the mending process to begin within a relationship.

Eliminating "sticks and stones" requires a decision of the heart and the willingness to speak life by speaking forgiveness and speaking reconciliation. How do we do this? When it comes to speaking relationally, the admonition is very basic -Keep it simple and keep it real.

First, don't wait for the "right moment" or for the right atmosphere. Often, taking the first step to reconcile can feel awkward and that can lead to procrastination and avoidance but it is important to speak. Do not allow long periods of time to pass before approaching your brother/sister. Prolonged offenses can deepen. The sooner you speak to the person, the better. Second, be certain that you are sincere in your heart and then politely ask to speak with the person. Third, speak clearly and, again be sincere. If you need forgiveness, admit your offense and ask for forgiveness and then ask what steps you can take to make restitution or what you can do to help begin the restoration process. If someone is asking you for forgiveness, listen carefully to the request for forgiveness and respond sincerely. You may not be able to gush with affection or use many flowery words but a verbal response is important. Silence at this point is like a stone and can further weaken the relationship. Speaking forthrightly, simply and earnestly can be used by the Holy Spirit to minister healing to hearts that are broken, hurting or offended.

Lastly, when you are faced with needing to mend a relationship, remind the person or persons involved in the exchange of your love for them. Perhaps, you are not accustomed to speaking about love or saying the words, "I love you" to another person. I am not suggesting that you carelessly throw around the words, "I love you", but I believe that God who is Love, wants us to share His love with one another. He is the One who gives us genuine love for one another and His love for us is what enables us to love one another. He does not want us to wait until we reach some kind of point of perfection before we begin confessing our love for one another in healthy, meaningful ways. It is great to demonstrate our love by buying gifts, showing acts of kindness etc... but <u>let us not forget to say it to one another</u>. (For clarity sake and in keeping with what promotes Godly relationships, I am speaking about pure, Godly, brotherly, sisterly love and kindness.) Love confession can be healing, restoring, redeeming and reconciling. Speaking agape love is definitely speaking life; a very powerful expression of care and concern.

Ultimately, let's be agents of change and get rid of those sticks and stones! Look for opportunities to say "Wow, I really appreciate your thoughtfulness. I love and appreciate you!". And, remember to be intentional and clear in saying, "I need to ask you to forgive me and allow me to take steps toward restoring our relationship. Would you please forgive me?" And, finally, remember the verbal response helps to close the gap, so a simple reply of "Yes, I forgive you and you can take the following steps toward restoration..." are words that are so vital in helping us to build relationship. Yes, redemptive and reconciling words, like a soothing balm help to restore and heal the wounded spirit.

Chapter Two

PROCLAIMING, DECREEING AND SPEAKING GOD'S WORD

I have proclaimed the good news of righteousness

in the great assembly (Psalm 40:10)

Pro' claim...To speak publicly, to make an official announcement and to state in such a way that the contents of the statement are unmistakable, and plainly declared. Proclamation is an important act in both the natural and spiritual sense. The results of proclaiming can be lasting and profound. Both terms, proclaiming and decreeing have significant implications for Christians, practitioners of God's Word. As the Scriptures explain, "Faith comes by hearing and hearing by the Word of God. How can they hear except the preacher preach and how can he preach except he be sent."(Romans 10: 17, 15). God's Word is the Divinely inspired direction and wisdom for His people. God gave His Word and He gave instructions as to how He planned for us to engage His Word. He has instructed us to read His Word; read His Word while we are alone; read His Word corporately; read His Word at informal settings; read His Word at formal settings...God also has instructed us to speak His Word and He has instructed us to speak It in specific ways. Because God's Word is authoritative, He wants us to speak authoritatively. God has told us to proclaim His

Word. Let's unpack this a little more. Why proclaim? Proclaim to whom? And, Proclaim when?

Proclaiming God's Word In The Context Of Our Personal Lives

For some Christians, proclaiming God's Word on Sundays and during worship services is an expected act of corporate fellowship. We stand during the public reading of the Word, say Amen after the reader completes the reading and engage in public affirmation of faith through the corporate reading of litanies and congregational readings. Yet, we somehow mistakenly believe that our conversational speech should be different. If Scripture is appropriate for Sunday worship then why isn't it appropriate for Monday conversation over coffee with friends and acquaintances. I'm not suggesting that we become Scripture record-

ings and talk in monotone sound bites. We should

respond to our neighbors and co-workers etc...

appropriately. But, can't we do more to share

Christ with others by simply sharing His Word.

For instance when others complain about the

weather, isn't that an opportunity to say, "You

know there is a verse in the Bible that says, "This

is the day the Lord has made, I will decide to

rejoice and be glad in it" (Psalm 118:24). Perhaps,

you will even offer the listeners a new paradigm -

a new way of looking at each day as a creation of

God and a new opportunity to choose to be glad

about each day.

Complaints, critical barbs and jabs or even

sophisticated expressions of doubt and despair

should not be met with agreement by a listening

Christian. There is an adage which states that

"silence gives consent". While this is not always the case, because sometimes it is the best choice to keep silent, in many instances, we are silent and our silence is like a stroke of affirmation to the speaker's words. I'm reminded of an acquaintance who is an avid cigarette smoker and when confronted, the person exclaimed, "We all are going to die from something, right?!". Responding with silence in this instance is the same as saying "Yep, you are right. I agree with you". But that is not all my agreement is confirming. My silence could be saying, 'since we are all going to die from 'something', it might as well be cigarette smoking.' Nothing could be further from the truth. First, we are not all going to "die from something". We know that death is inevitable but death by sickness is a presumption and not necessarily true. Second, in spite of the inevitability of death, God never meant for us to live with a defeatist attitude. He means for us to live! Since abundant life is the goal, why speak death? Why speak opposite to the plan of God for our lives. Speak life and live!

Confronting the spirit of despair couched in the words of a cynic is incredibly important. Because words have spiritual influence and attitudes, mindsets can be transferred without the listener realizing what is happening. If we don't answer back the inferences of such words, we leave ourselves vulnerable to agreeing with or even becoming what is spoken. Often, this is a challenge because our acquaintances can sometimes speak so fast, offering us little room to inject counterpoints which would reflect a Godly point of view. When I find myself in this situation, I am tempted to think, Oh well, I am not the one speaking. Resisting the temptation I can pray inwardly and ask the Holy Spirit to show me what to say and how to say it. I can seek God's guidance for the moment. I can also intercede for the individual who is speaking in such a way and I can, if necessary, remove myself from the situation but not without remembering that God loves everyone and he wants us to have the same compassion. God will give us ways to resist and confront sin and yet maintain love for the person who needs God's grace as do all of us.

I recall attending a workshop at a conference. The workshop leader was very knowledgeable but used extreme profanity and vulgarity in his presentation. It seemed as if speaking this way was a part of his daily speaking personality. Almost every sentence was syncopated with an expletive. At one point I stepped out of the workshop and prayed silently, "Lord, even though this workshop would be beneficial to my job, you know I do not want to listen to the abusive language. What should I do?" The Lord surprisingly prodded my heart to return to the workshop and assured me that I would have an opportunity to express my disfavor with his use of profane language. After about ten minutes more, the workshop ended because the workshop leader wanted the participants to have time to ask questions in informal small groups. For research purposes, he also wanted us to fill out a detailed evaluation of the workshop. One of the evaluation questions asked, 'Did the presenter use appropriate language during the presentation?'. As you can imagine, I was able to write my response to that question and explain that as a Christian I believe his use of profanity was offensive and distracting.

To better explain, let's consider the following example. I hadn't seen Mrs. Baker in at least five years (Her name is changed to preserve her identity). She was standing in line at the book shop in the shopping mall. I had gone into the book store to browse while my sons shopped at a popular sports store. I approached her happily, "Mrs. Baker! It is so good to see you." "Oh my goodness, it is good to see you!" she replied. She was still tall and lean. Her slender form gave no hint of her age. I could see a bit of change in her face and her close-cropped afro was now more gray than black but she was still spry and appeared strong. "You look great. How are you?" I asked. And that question opened the door for a significant shift of focus. Her face tightened and her shoulders drooped, "Oh, I don't know. I've been dealing with some impossible situations...". For the next few moments she continued to explain her situation was, in her words, "hopeless". This example points to a typical, everyday exchange. What seems like a harmless reporting of difficulties in the natural becomes a kind of confirmation in the spiritual realm that things are going according to plan. Which plan? If the confession is negative, the enemy acts as though his plan is progressing (we know that ultimately, the enemy has already been defeated, but he acts as if he still has a chance of winning). If the confession is a proclamation using the Word of God, the enemy is frustrated and the Lord is praised and glorified. When we praise the Lord, we, in effect, give Him more room to work in our lives. We allow the plan of God to operate in our lives. And, the plan of God, which is always about shaping us more and more into the image of Christ and building Godly character in our lives and advancing the purposes of God, is going to happen with or without our participation. We need to desire to be a part of His plan in the earth and desire for His plan be a part of our lives. Returning to the conversation with my friend, Mrs. Baker, how could her confession have been spoken differently so that she could have felt free to express her difficulty and yet proclaim hopefulness in Christ? Mrs. Baker is just an example, but proclaiming our hope in Christ even when situations are difficult is for all of us. This can be done by acknowledging the problem, acknowledging that we are praying for a solution, speaking the Word over the situation and then expecting God to respond.

When we proclaim God's Word, even in daily conversation, we are making it public and official that this is what I live by. I do not live by my circumstances, I live by faith in the Word of God. In essence, I live publicly and privately by the Word of God.

When we speak life, we live out a Scriptural pattern of problem-solving. Here it is again: Acknowledge the problem, pray for the solution, speak the Word and expect God to answer:

1. Realistic understanding of the problem at hand   (Problem)
2.) Expression of Prayer to God for the solution to the problem   (Prayer)
3.) Expression of faith in God by speaking God's Word over the problem   (Speaking the Word)
4.) Expression of the believed Outcome (Expectation)

Why It Is Important To <u>Confess</u> That We Have Prayed and Continue to Pray For A Particular Situation

It is more important that we say what we are doing in response to a problem or challenge than to simply say the problem. This is the entryway into faith. Often, we don't want to speak about what we are doing in response to a problem. There are various reasons for this reticence.

*We may feel embarrassed that we have the problem in the first place

*We may feel helpless

*We may not be able to do what we want to do to help the situation

*We may fear that what we are able to do is inadequate

*We are angry that our response was ignored in the past

*We may be frustrated that our warning was unheeded

*We may be upset that the problem is to no fault of our own and is costing us a great deal of emotional, maybe even, financial pain and suffering
*We may simply feel hurt

And there are many other scenarios that can cause us to keep our confession at a weak, low whisper. A whimpering confession is better than no confession (after all mustard-seed faith works!)

But the quality of the confession is critical to the effectiveness of the confession because out of the abundance of the heart the mouth speaks. If we have little faith, we speak little about our faith and a lot about our fears. What is abundant in the heart is what spills out into our conversation. Once again, I want to emphasize the importance of saying your response to a problem, not just saying the problem. This means that God wants us to be intentional about praying about the problem and then saying that we are praying about it. The words, 'I'm praying about it' represent a strong and powerful statement of faith to believers and strong and powerful witness to unbelievers. It is more than cliché. When we say we are praying about it, we should understand that we are saying we are in dialog with God about the matter and confident in His ability and willingness to help us.

WHAT SHOULD OUR BEHAVIOUR BE WHEN WE ARE "PRAYING ABOUT IT"?

Several years ago, I served on jury duty and, after hearing the case presented by both sides, the prosecutor and the defense, we were sequestered or confined to a single room in the judicial complex of that town. The room seemed bare, even austere with a long conference table, chairs, several windows with blinds, a water cooler and paper cups and several boxes of tissue. There was one dictionary on a single book stand at the back of the room. We were given specific instructions and a stern warning not to talk about the case with anyone else other than fellow jury members also in the room at the time. We were not to call friends and relatives and/or e-mail, face book or twitter with others for the duration of the process. We could go home to our families at night but we had made a pledge that we would not discuss the court case even with our spouses and family members.

While the jury was going through this process, we were considered in active deliberations or evaluation of the two sides represented. The judge did not want anything to sway our thinking unfairly or unconstitutionally.

Let me share another example, I was asked by a major denomination to help mediate a deeply divisive conflict within the regional body of this denomination. Emotions were raw and conciliatory talks had ended in gridlock again and again. Someone had the idea of inviting a Communications person to listen to the conflict

ਪਹਿਲਾਂ

and help the group arrive at an agreeable solution. Before the official meeting, the denomination representative met with me and explained their approach. She explained that if I agreed to mediate the conflict, I should be willing to suspend any and all conversation about the conflict, the denomination and any surrounding topics with outsiders, including my husband. The rules of mediation in this case considered that during active "talks", I needed to maintain an attitude of optimism and state only that "we are talking about it" or " we are expecting an agreeable solution".

In other words, it was not acceptable for me to function in the role of mediator, one who communicates to the group certain steps toward the solution, and then express doubt about whether or not the group can or cannot reach an agreement.

In much the same way, when we are praying through a situation with the Lord, we are in "deliberation" with Him. We are in "talks" with Him and we really should not say words that cast doubt on the plausibility of a solution. Of course, prayer is not mediation or deliberation in the strict sense, but the point is the attitudes which accompany judicious processes such as these can teach us a lot about the kind of attitudes we should have when we are asking the Lord to work out difficult problems, challenges and conflicts in our lives. And, even when the source of your conflict is the pain in a loved one's life, you can ask the Lord to resolve that conflict because it is effecting you and causing you dissonance and unrest within your soul.

When trouble spots arise, I may share the problem from an informational standpoint, but more importantly I should take a "God and I are talking" posture. I am not free to say very much about this case until the Judge has His final say. I am in the midst of deliberations, and spiritually, I am sequestered (set aside) until the breakthrough comes. Too much talk might cloud my thinking and ability to hear from the Lord. Other people might mean well, but they might speak out of their own emotions or bias. This will in turn bias my openness to the Holy Spirit and His direction for me in the situation. It takes quiet to hear from God. And time. Let patience have her perfect turn.

One more thing about mediation, even though I was restricted in my freedom to talk with others, I was given full access to the parties involved. Even if I wanted to call an early morning or late night meeting, (with some respect for the participants' schedules, of course) I could do that. I could call at almost any time and speak with key partici- pants and ask for clarification. The jury could ask for review of documents, photos and any evidence submitted in the formal presentation of the case.

One of the things we could not do is that we could not hurry the process. We spent a great deal of time waiting. We were even dismissed early at some point because of missing documents or legal technicalities which needed redress among the attorneys. We could not rush the process! And, during the process, all of our needs were well provided. Although the work was arduous, the administrators of the court took full respon- sibility for our care. We were provided breakfast and lunch, plenty of bottled water and bathroom breaks. When you are in deliberations, awaiting an answer from the Court, you are restricted from talking with those outside the case, but then the Court assumes all responsibility for your needs, even affording us, in addition to our meals, a small stipend each day.

When we enter "talks" with God (prayer) and we are deliberating over a specific concern, God takes responsibility for us in ways that we can't even imagine. He provides all of the emotional and physical support we need while we are going through the process. And, we can talk with the Lord as much as we desire, whenever we desire. We can go back to the Lord and request review of His Word (Lord, what did you say about...?). We can open the Bible and re-read the evidence. This is why it is important to take good notes when the Lord is speaking either through His servants during the preaching/teaching of the Word or in our quiet time of devotions. While we may be restricted in saying a lot of extraneous words to everybody else, we are perfectly free to speak at any time with our Advocate, the One to whom we are praying and trusting for the answer and solution.

Some of us exhibit what I call talk-dependency. We can't stop talking. We think we have to explain and explain and supply details and on and on...

God is The Almighty Judge. He does not need us to "help" Him with details and descriptions. "In quietness and confidence shall be your strength" (Isaiah 30: 15).

When we are in "talks" with God, let us wait on Him and allow Him to walk us through the process. Let's give the process the proper environment for solution. This might mean marking out a secure space, not in secrecy but in quiet - there's a difference. A space where there are no competing voices and opinions. This might require you to spend a little more time in prayer and meditation. You might even need to spend some time fasting and seeking the Lord. You will not be disappointed. The Lord will minister to you at your point of need.

Proclaiming God's Word In The Corporate Worship Service

To this point, we have explored how important it is to proclaim the Word of God in personal settings such as at home, work, between neighbors. Now, let's turn our attention to the proclamation of the Word in corporate worship. Why is there always a sermon or teaching during Christian services? Are there do's and don'ts for proclaiming God's Word during services? Finally, what should the goal be for proclamation during services? The following Scripture was mentioned earlier, but let's look at it again

In Romans 10:14-15 the context is fully explained.

> *How then shall they call on Him in whom they have not believed? And how shall they believe in Him of whom they have not heard? And how shall they hear without a preacher? And how shall they preach unless they are sent?*

The expressed purpose of a Christian preacher's assignment is to ensure that we "hear" the Gospel and thereby believe in Jesus Christ. The goal of preaching is proclaiming the message of Jesus Christ so that people receive it, repent of their sins and accept Jesus Christ as personal

Lord and Savior. In the words of Bible Scholar and Author, Dr. Haddon Robinson, "To the New Testament writers, preaching stands as the event through which God works" (Robinson, 2005). Preaching edifies, builds up and inspires faith and courage in Jesus Christ. How can this be done without the continual proclaiming of the Word of God. Scripture supports the necessity for weekly meeting times of worship and sharing of the Word. It is found in Exodus 20: 8-10. *Remember the Sabbath day to keep it Holy. Six days you shall labor and do all your work but the seventh day is the Sabbath of the Lord your God.* Although there are doctrinal and denominational differences concerning the Sabbath day and which day of the week should actually be observed, most Christians will agree that setting aside at least one day of the week for worship, fellowship and rest is a Biblical mandate. Part of 'keeping it Holy' is meeting together for worship, exhortation, hearing from God and having one's faith in God strengthened. While music and breaking bread together (eating), sharing in community activities and organizing good will projects are all great, there is that one question so fundamental to the purpose of the weekly service, *how can they hear* without the preaching or proclaiming of God's Word?

Hebrews 10:24-25 says *"And let us consider one another in order to stir up love and good works, not forsaking the assembling of ourselves together as is the manner of some, but exhorting one another and so much more as you see the day approaching."* This Scripture reminds us of the fact that the Church is the 'Body' of Christ and we are all members of that Body. We have a responsibility to one another. Part of that responsibility is establishing a recognizable identity in the earth as those who belong to Christ. Therefore, it is important that we publicly identify with Christ and publicly state His Word; His statues; His ordinances; His commandments. And, it is equally important that we live out His mandate to us, to love one another - with deep, agape love. By this will all people know that we are Christ's disciples - Christ's followers. Fulfillment of these goals require a public sphere and intentional interaction. How should proclamation take place in corporate worship? Prayerfully. Reverently. Those who are involved in speaking during a worship service must be absolutely convinced of the sacred responsibility of what they are doing. They must not hypocritically involve themselves in facilitating any portion of the service but rather serve out of hearts filled with devotion, repentance and humility in the Lord. But, God's servants should not be timid or apologetic for sharing God's Word. This is why it is proclaiming. The tenor of preaching, rather quiet in nature or strong-voiced and robust should be forthright. The Holy Spirit gives the preacher a Holy boldness and resolve of faith. With the spirit of 'I know in whom I believe and am fully persuaded', the preacher proclaims the Word of God.

The responsibility of the audience is to prayerfully receive the Word. We prepare ourselves for the Word by praying before it is shared, praying while it is shared and praying after it is shared that we will obey what we have heard.

WHAT DOES IT MEAN TO DECREE

To decree means to give an authoritative order which is backed by the force of law or legislation. The Latin root, 'decernere' means to decide. The noun form, a decree, is the stated decision of an authoritative rule which establishes a matter and all associations with the thing established. A decree is an order, a decision determining what is to be done by all parties involved. Who has the right to decree? Do you and I? On what basis can we make a decree? When and how are we able to make a decree? And, to whom shall we decree?

Understanding the function and role of the decree will change your prayer life and your expectation from God.

To begin, we as members of the Body of Christ have authority, spiritual authority in the Name of Jesus Christ. This means we have power in the Name of Jesus, by faith, to do the things God wants done on the earth. The way that we "do" what God wants us to do is by first speaking what God wants done, by declaring prophetically that God's will shall happen. When we recognize an injustice such as (spiritual and natural) oppression, imprisonment, bondage, lack, thievery, assault, we have spiritual authority to go before the Heavenly Judge and petition the Heavenly Court. Jesus, our Advocate petitions on our behalf and the Holy Spirit transfers our prayers and often, unintelligent groanings to the Court. After petitioning, we then have spiritual authority to make decrees for or against the matter and the substance of the decree rests in God's heart concerning the matter. Once we decree, speak out God's heart, we release the ministering angels to go forth and execute that which has been decreed. There is such awesome power in this privilege that is given to the faithful children of God. The enemy keeps us tongue-tied in this area because he does not want us to discover who we really are and our authority in Christ.

If you think carefully about God's perspective of words and speech, you will agree that He counts the capacity for language as a very, very important spiritual activity. Go back to Genesis Chapters One and Two. Chapter One, verse two states, "The earth was without form and void... And the Spirit of God was hovering over the face of the waters. (Verse three) "Then God said, "Let there be light" and there was light." Before each concurrent act of creation, God spoke. He spoke and there was light; He spoke and there was fir-

mament; He spoke and the waters appeared...
until His creation was complete.

God being Almighty could have created the
various forms of being and life without any
spoken word. The fact that He spoke and it was
so, models for us, the spiritual order and relationship between speech and action. God put this
dynamic capacity within us. He means for our
hearts to be so in tune with His will and the meditation of our spirit to be so filled with His Word
that when we speak, we will be speaking what He
wants and He will hasten to perform it. God never
meant there to be a disconnect between a person's
inner life and his/her spoken words. What we
meditate upon is what we end up speaking. Out
of the abundance of the heart, the mouth speaks.
Be careful to recognize your authority in Christ
and be sensitive to the Holy Spirit's promptings.

When the Lord reveals His will to you, confirm it by His Word and then speak it, decree it and trust God for the results. The key is to make sure that what you are desiring or looking to see done is truly the will of God. God is so good. He will prosper His Word!

THOUGHT CHECK....What are you praying through right now? What is the major situation in your life that is heaviest on your heart and you know it is only God who can solve the problem?

Take a moment to write it down and ask God to give you a renewed commitment to pray about it differently. From this point, you are going to pray about it to the Lord more and talk about it less to others. When you do speak about this issue, you are going to Proclaim, Decree or Speak God's Word over it. Be specific, be intentional and be stead-

fast. Let God Work it out.

Chapter Three

Imparting, Teaching. Training, Speaking and Mentoring

He gave some to be apostles, some prophets,

some evangelists, and some pastors and teachers

for the equipping of the saints for the work of

ministry for the edifying of the body of Christ...

that we should no longer be children tossed to

and fro and carried about with every wind of

doctrine...but speaking the truth in love may

grow up in all things into Him who is the head -

Christ... (Ephesians 4: 11 -15)

W hen is the last time you taught someone how to do something...something you can do well...something you love to do and other people love to watch you or receive the results of your ability or talent? Perhaps, you might think that you haven't really shown anyone how to do anything special...No spectacular demonstrations for a mesmerized protégé...No complexly revealed explanation falling upon curious and easily impressed ears. Perhaps not, but I believe there is a significant portion of you reading this chapter who have children. Have you ever shown your children how to wash dishes, make their beds, throw a baseball, fold a shirt or bake a cake? Haven't there been times when you helped your children with homework or special projects such as learning how to play a musical instrument, building a birdhouse or completing a science model for a science fair. What about the first time you played Scrabble or Monopoly with your child, niece or nephew? While you were teaching them in those moments, you were, in effect, actively mentoring them.

Mentoring is the art of training another in the likeness of a mentor or guide. God means for us to use our energies, abilities and talents in the training and development of others coming along behind us. One of the factors that will help us to freely give in this area of mentoring is the remembrance of how other people mentored, taught and encouraged us when we were young in the faith. There are several characteristics of Godly mentoring:

Mentoring is generational

Mentoring is cyclical

Mentoring is up close and personal

Mentoring is teaching by example

When we mentor someone, we have the opportunity of teaching by example...of speaking into their lives by our actions and our words. The Godly mentor will also pray for his/her mentee and cherish the opportunity of being a part of the Holy Spirit's work of Grace in the lives of others.

Impartation - The Importance of Transferring God's Purpose, Plan & Anointing

When I speak of impartation in this chapter, I am referring to the spiritual, emotional and attitudinal transfer carried by words between individuals and groups that effects behavior. Biblical teaching explains how anointing and the stirring up of spiritual gifts can be imparted by the laying on of hands. While I believe this is still active in the Church today, my focus is primarily the impartation that comes by spoken word. While laying on of hands is typically done within the context of a worship service, impartation by words happens both ceremonially and informally. It is relational and often, we are even unaware that impartation by words is taking place.

To see this principle at work in the natural, consider the Biblical story of Joshua:

After the death of Moses the servant of the Lord, it came to pass that the Lord spoke to Joshua the son of Nun, Moses' assistant...Now therefore arise go over this Jordan, you and all this people to the land which I am giving to them...Every place that the sole of your foot will tread upon I have given you as I said to Moses...No man shall be able to stand before you...I will not leave you nor forsake you. Be strong and of good courage...This Book of the law shall not depart from your mouth but you shall meditate in it day and night that you may observe to do according to all that is written in it. For then you will make your way prosperous and then you will have good success. (Joshua1:1- 8)

This was the Word from the Lord to Joshua and this is what he communicated to the Israelites (Vs 10 - 15) and this is how they responded:

So they answered Joshua saying, "All that you command us we will do and wherever you send us we will go" (Joshua 1: 16)

After the Lord spoke to Joshua, he spoke to the people and by his words, he imparted courage and hopefulness to them. They were resolved and ready to follow him. When I read the Joshua

Chapter one, I can see the importance and role of strong leadership. Moses had died. A whole nation of people had just come through a traumatic shift in their destiny. Having been displaced and yet having gone through such awesome deliverance as the parting of the Red Sea, they were yet at another crossroad, desperately in need of direction. Joshua speaks to them and they are encouraged and re-focused. To strengthen this discussion on impartation, I invited several seminarians to share insight about impartation.

From Bishop Joseph Quainoo

Impartation is a transference of grace and/or spirit to enable or to empower others; to impact them or to influence them either negatively or positively. When it is genuine, proper, it is from God and intended to equip His people or the work of ministry and to glorify God. It is designed to move them from the place of inability or mediocrity or weakness into a place of effective working; a place of excellence in ministry; a place of exemplary lifestyle; in short, a place where the believer glorifies God.

A transference in the spiritual sense, the Holy spirit uses the uniqueness of people to accomplish great things in ministry...the emphasis is on being empowered. The recipient has to walk in faith; they have to walk in holiness; they have to walk in obedience to God; they still have to line their life up with Scripture.

A classic example is with Elijah & Elisha & Gehazi, not that there had not been an impartation but Gehazi was still driven by greed; still ruled by the spirit of selfishness. This could explain why that even serving under a great man like Elisha, he was influenced in such a manner that he could lie and pursue worldly gain and end

up being cursed with leprosy. (II Kings chapter

5:20 ff).

And Paul said to Timothy fan the gift that was

imparted unto you through the laying on of hands.

There had been an impartation unto Timothy but

had grown dull and Paul was admonishing him to

stir up the gift. Biblically, blessing a person was the

speaking of life through words. Another example

is Goliath confronting David - trying to transfer

the spirit of fear, but David understood that prin-

ciple and reversed that curse back to Goliath and

defeated Goliath

Every time Goliath taunted Israel, he was transferring the spirit of fear. The people were gripped with fear and no one would confront Goliath.

Yet another example is of Isaac blessing Jacob and Esau...it wasn't so much the laying on of hands, it was more the speaking of words. It was later when Jacob was blessing the sons of Joseph that we see the laying on of hands becoming prominent.

Speaking blessing is a type of impartation.

From Rev. Dr. Fredericka Wilson

Impartation from one Christian to another is something that is found throughout the Scriptures. It can be spoken or it can be the laying on of hands. In the Old Testament, fathers would bless their children by speaking a blessing and laying hands. This was a transfer of the blessing from the father to his descendants. God touched the mouth of Moses. God imparted his words to him. Through prophets, kings were anointed for the service to God.

In the New Testament, Jesus imparted to his disciples. He imparted with spoken words, but he also breathed on them. In Acts, you find many examples of impartation through spoken words. Paul imparted blessings and encouraged the young Christian church.

From Pastor Troy Edwards

Our faithful, omnipotent, and sovereign God has delegated responsibility to men and women from the day that He created them (Gen. 2:26-27).

It has always been God's desire to bless but He has chosen to do this primarily through others, primarily His delegated authority. This was a risky thing that God chose to do since He also gave men and women the ability to not act as His desired channels of imparting blessing unto others.

Throughout Scripture God has delegated the responsibility to Patriarchs to impart blessing to their progeny, for rulers to impart blessing to their people, and for spiritual leaders to impart blessing to the people God has given them charge over. This has been primarily done in Scripture by means of laying on of hands and speaking author-itative words. The words spanned from everything from spiritual gifts to material prosperity, health, long life and numerous descendants. Those who received these impartations took these words seri-ously. In one case, Jacob was reluctant to follow his mother's advice to deceive his father Isaac in case his father would curse him rather than bless him. His brother Esau cried and sobbed and even vowed vengeance upon Jacob for stealing the blessing he felt rightfully belonged to him from an impartation of his father.

Why such a big to do over "words" if there was no power in them to bring things to pass? The Bible tells us that life and death is in the power of the tongue (Prov. 18:21). The old adage, "sticks and stones may break my bones but words will never hurt me" do not contain any real truth. Words can bless and they can curse. Words can heal and they can bring wars. Major world wars were started over words. Words have power to impart blessing or curse.

God has not limited this power to impart only to leaders. He has also called men and women to impart blessing to one another regardless of social, political, or spiritual stature. It is God's desire to bless, but His primary means of blessing people is through other people: *"Give, and it shall be given unto you; good measure, pressed down, and shaken together, and running over, **shall men give** into your bosom"* (Luke 6:38). Again, God took a very large risk in expecting His perfect will to be done through fallible men, especially when He created them with the capacity to do the very opposite of that which He desires them to do.

Mature men and women of God have learned to pray for their friends, family, co-workers, neighbors, and fellow church goers and have declared God's blessings over them. These are people who have caught the true loving heart of God and, like Him, want to impart love and blessing to others.

Chapter Four

No Weapon - Speak Victory!

No weapon formed against you shall prosper and

every tongue which rises against you in judgment

you shall condemn (Isaiah 54:17)

There are many things that can crush
a person's ambition and desire to suc-
ceed. Natural disasters, the loss of a loved one
or financial challenge are all examples of difficulties which are hard to overcome. But, there is yet
another category of challenges which presents a

particular difficulty to the person who is walking by faith, that is, controlling what we say; our own confession. How many times have you spoken defeat even before beginning a task?

Biblical confession and Godly expectation spoken out loud is one of our most important spiritual weapons and line of defense- why do we as Christians lay down our weapons and concede defeat at the slightest sign of battle? "For the weapons of our warfare are not carnal but mighty to the pulling down of strongholds" (II Corinthians 10:4). And spoken confession of the Word is one of the 'weapons of our warfare'.

In basic communication studies, there is a phenomenon called the self-fulfilling prophecy. This describes the likelihood of an outcome of a situation, task or event to turn out as predicted. Many intelligent, well-respected individuals will privately avoid stating claims of victory or making certain utterances before a contest, a presentation etc... because they are convinced that if "I talk about it too much, it will turn out bad". Or, "every time I say it's going to be a sunny day, it rains, so I'll say it will probably rain and then maybe the sun will shine." These "good luck" statements and thoughts and maneuvers are an offense to God. The Bible says "we walk by faith and not by sight". We are to live by faith and "faith is the substance of things hoped for and the evidence of things unseen". And, "without faith it is impossible to please God for he who comes to God must believe that He is and that He is a rewarder of those who diligently seek Him" (Hebrews 11:6). Therefore, we are to speak clearly, forthrightly and specifically about our intentions and desires recognizing that our words have power and spiritual impact. We must understand that before an act or event can take place in the realm of the natural it must be declared, proclaimed and/or decreed in the spiritual. The natural reality that we experience is a residual effect of what has already taken place in the spiritual - a physical manifestation of the spiritual. This is a very profound principle which many Christians ignore, are ignorant of or take for granted. Furthermore, we underestimate the power that we have as Christians to speak and thereby exercise our God-given authority.

To clarify, let us consider the parameters of this truth. Let us establish what speaking victoriously does not mean and then explain in fuller detail what we do mean when we say, "speak victory". Keep in mind that speaking victoriously is a command and invitation given to us by our Lord. It is a form of authority and a way of exercising authority. I John 5:4 says "For whatever is born of God overcomes the world. And this is the victory that has overcome the world - our faith." Jesus wants us to spcak in accordance with this faith - *Overcoming Faith!* We speak that which we believe and that which we believe is grounded in the reality of Christ, our Savior, our Advocate, our Victory! In Revelation chapter 12 the enemy, satan, is described as "the accuser of our brethren". The devil's accusations are an affront to Christ, our High Priest and Redeemer, The One who has settled our sin debt. When we accept Jesus Christ as our Savior, we are free from the debt of sin and do not stand accused, but rather exonerated. The enemy acting as if the redemptive work of Jesus Christ is of none effect, continues right on with his accusations against the people of God, "accusing them before our God day and night" vs. 10. Now, the Bible says that the enemy "has been cast down" vs. 10. We are to walk in the authority of our freedom based on the truth of God's Word according to vs. 11. "And they overcame him by the blood of the Lamb and by the word of their testimony". This means we are to say what Jesus has done and agree with that truth. We are not to agree with the accusation and the lies of the enemy for he is the deceiver and the "father of lies". We are overcomers because of the Blood that was shed by Jesus our Savior on the Cross at Calvary. And we apply that truth with the word of our testimony...A testimony is the result of "speaking"! To testify is to speak victory! Tell of His Goodness! Shout to the Heavens! Proclaim it from the rooftops! When the woman at the well was confronted by Jesus with her own need for a Savior, and after realizing who she was talking to - that it was Jesus Himself, she ran into town and began to *testify,* "Come see a man who told me about myself".

What follows is a list of ways in which speaking in authority can be misused or mishandled:

*First, speaking in authority does not mean speaking by the flesh to fulfill desires based in fantasy or selfish/self-centered pursuit.

*Second, speaking in authority does not mean speaking in arrogance and pride with the motive of drawing attention to one's abilities, talents and possessions

*Third, speaking in authority does not mean using words to control; words to dominate another person in unhealthy ways; to force, manipulate or subdue under your will.

*Fourth, speaking in authority does not mean cajoling, ridiculing or harassing another person with the expressed purpose of causing that person to "give in" to your control.

*Fifth, speaking in authority does not mean emotional baiting or psychological trickery in order to "get" another person to act the way we think he/she should act. This includes exploiting, harassing and playing upon the vulnerability of others

*Sixth, speaking in authority does not mean coercion by force, the use of fear of consequences or threat. When this boundary is crossed, it is particularly dangerous because criminal behavior can be the result of violating another person in this way, such as in the case of rape or assault.

These patterns are all negative reversals of what God meant to be a blessing to each of us individually and to the Body of Christ. God intended for authority to be an expression of order and leadership - servant leadership (See Robert Greenleaf). So what does it mean to speak in authority. What follows is a list of ways in which speaking in authority can be a blessing.

*First, the believer who speaks in authority gives clear direction to those following him/her. The goal is to lead, not drive or harshly demand others. One of the first works of the Holy Spirit in the life of the person who becomes a Christian is the work of conviction of sin. In fact, the Holy Spirit convicts individuals of sin even before they become a Christian and convinces the person of the need for salvation; the need for Jesus Christ as personal Lord and Savior. In essence, this need, when acknowledged, is full admittance of the fact that without Christ "I am lost". What is it that I need? Direction! I need the Lord to help me to make the right choices; wise choices and Godly decisions. I need the Lord to help me manage my life. This humility is difficult, yes, impossible, without the work of the Holy Spirit.

*Speaking in authority means speaking in ways that are healing and ministering to the soul of the listener.

*Speaking in authority is prophetic speaking

*Speaking in authority can be the appropriation of discipline, rebuke and correction

*Speaking in authority is exhortation

*Speaking in authority is the revealing of vision. Write the vision and make it plain that those who see it might understand" Habakkuk 2:2.

Giving place for proper, Godly authority in my life is accepting God's help for me in all areas of my life. The antithesis of this yielding to the Holy Spirit is an unfortunate boastfulness and pride. The Word of Gods says that pride goes before destruction and a haughty spirit before a fall. In this instance, before I can be helped, I must first admit that I need help. Attitudes which say "I can do it myself" or "I can make it on my own" are wrong attitudes which lead to downfalls and pitfalls and unnecessary hardness along the journey of life. When we accept that we need God's help and we need to be led, then we accept God's spiritual authority (See Watchman Nee). Godly authority is God's answer to me and my need for direction.

Why is accepting authority from the Lord such a difficulty for many believers? As stated earlier it is a problem of the heart and consequence of pride - a spiritual problem. There is another problem that wars against our ability to accept the Lord's provision of authority and that is the issue of trust. The Word of God teaches us to place our trust in the Lord. For many believers, hearing from the Lord is an "iffy" circumstance, a hit or miss happenstance. When they hear God's Word proclaimed, they do not ask the Lord to anoint their ears to hear and receive the Word that is being preached. In fact, there are many distractions that vie for our attention during the preaching of God's Word. Often we are drawn to recall our past or most recent pursuits and involvements. The Preacher's clothing or style of speaking may distract us. We can be easily wooed by other things which seem pressing. All of these affects combine to create an atmosphere that is not conducive to hearing the Word of God and respecting the proclaiming of His Word as authoritative.

It is extremely important for us to realize that when the Word of God is being taught, proclaimed, sung or shared, we who are listening are hearing the literal, live, transformative Word of God. That Word is authoritative and ought to be given immediate attention and received without doubt, hesitance or second-guessing. Along with a respect for God's Word comes the respect for the messenger- the preacher/teacher, singer or speaker who is delivering the Message. We must resist the temptation to think of other things during the proclaiming of God's Word.

This is not to say that we are wrong to inquire about the ethics and soundness of a Preacher or Bible Teacher. He/She ought to be held to the highest Biblical standards of Godliness in doctrine as well as in lifestyle. For this reason, Church leaders and speakers should identify themselves when introduced to new audiences as Christians who have testimonies of lives of consistency and Holiness. But our main goal as listeners should be to receive the Word of the Lord as His Provision of direction and inspiration for us.

Chapter Five

The New Covenant - Speaking In Community

I remember working very hard delivering a sermon about the Christian perspective of financial prosperity. It was a lesson titled *God's Financial Provision For Us, His People.* I can recall how I felt after pouring out my heart and then listening as the moderator took the microphone after my sermon was over. Not only did the moderator not comment on the message, but candidly, the moderator "unpreached" my sermon by reminding the congregation how important it is to be content with the "little" amounts that God gives us. "Little becomes much when you place it in the Master's Hand...God never promised to supply all of our wants, just our needs." Are these true words? Yes.

Well, somewhat. The moderator's words spoken immediately after a sermon on God's provision were ill-timed and consequently counter-productive. I believe God wants us to maximize our sensitivity by stepping in time with the word for the moment. It reminds me of my experience during graduate school as an early morning worker at the campus café. The Café opened at 6a.m. and it was my sole responsibility to open the café at 5a.m. and ready the tables and serving stations for the breakfast rush hour. In order to arrive at my job on time, I had to walk 15 minutes from my campus apartment to the Student Union at the center of campus. Each morning without fail, the ROTC military cadets would be in the middle of one of their fitness drills...Hu - Two, Three, Four...Hu - Two, Three, Four. In complete unison they would monotone their chants and step in perfect rhythm together. TOGETHER.

I'm sure at 4:30a.m. all of the soldiers were not "feeling" the drill. Perhaps some were thinking privately that they could create a livelier song and lead the chant with more pizzazz. (If indeed one is able to achieve pizzazz at that hour in the morning). If they had followed their inclinations, they would have been out of order and duly chastised because perfectly good ideas would have been ill-timed and thus wrongly executed. The excellence of their drills can be attributed to, in part, their unity and display of oneness.

Likewise, Christians must learn the discipline of speaking together. TOGETHER. Speaking in community involves the sensitivity to what the Spirit of God is saying to the corporate Body and building on that Word...not introducing a counter word that, on its own, is true and relevant, but in the context of the moment could create confusion or voice disagreement with a previous Word (rather intentionally or unintentionally). God does not want us functioning in competition and creating dissonance or discordant sounds. We must learn the art of saying Amen and the importance of the supporting role. But this is not done through human means. Knowing when to speak, what to say and how to say it is part of the fruit of the Spirit produced in and through us as we obey Christ and live Spirit-filled and Spirit-led lives. In American culture, freedom of speech is the ultimate American right, and we believe, human right. And, as a patriotic American, I cherish the right to speak and to say what is on my mind without fear of reprisal, however, there are times when my cultural privilege must give way to the Spirit of God. Even though I have the right to speak, at times it might profit little if I do or it might be slightly off-base and thereby do greater harm than good. It is at these times, that the Holy spirit would have us examine ourselves and yield to Him, even our right to speak about the issue set before us. After all, what is the greater gain, to exert the personal right to speak or glorify God by waiting to speak or speaking to affirm what has been rightly said. We don't always have to be in a hurry to speak. We don't always have to be the one to set the record straight. We don't always have to explore all the angles of an option or topic of discussion. I've heard statements/justifications for ill-timed counter-comments such as "I just wanted everyone to know that there are other sides to the story." Or statements which are well-meaning but sow seeds of disunity, "Even though our Pastor has recommended that we make the first choice, I'd just like to remind everyone that we do have a second choice." In this context, if speaking is "speaking life" then making such counter-statements is "unspeaking". It can be disruptive, divisive and breed disharmony. It can stifle the life-giving thrust and potential of powerful effect resident within the Word that was first spoken. Picture this...A young boy standing in the median at a round-about intersection. One friend is on one side and another friend on the other... Let's imagine his name is Jeffrey. His friends are speaking to him one at a time.

"Jeffrey, cross over here. Turn left and come my way. I'll tell you when there are no cars coming. Just watch me."

And then from the other friend, "Jeffrey, you should cross to my side. Turn right and come my way" I'll tell you when there are no cars coming. Just watch me." What kind of dilemma does this present for Jeffrey. Both friends are shouting directions to him. Either choice could be a good choice, but he can only make one choice at the time. What if the two friends came together and both called him at the same time to help him cross toward one direction.

When we speak our voice should resonate with the Lord's message that is currently being spoken. We should not contest the authority of the Word. We should lovingly, but firmly, challenge false teaching and erroneous thinking. We should strongly raise our voices against oppression and abuse. But when our brother or sister is teaching Godly principles and there is no compromise or falsity in their presentation, we should not take issue with the message simply because we know equally plausible messages.

UNITY AS AN AID TO EFFECTIVENESS

God's Word teaches us that we as Christians should love one another and that "they", the world, will know us by our love. Publicly yielding the right of way to one another as we speak allows us to demonstrate this love. When the Word is spoken, there are several ways in which that Word is confirmed or disconfirmed. What follows is an assessment of **Confirmation Principles** - Ways in which a corporate Word can be confirmed by the body and **Disconfirmation Principles** - Ways

in which a corporate Word can be disconfirmed.

Confirmation Principles

1.) Inner witness of the Holy Spirit

2.) Verbal affirmation by individuals (*As in saying*

"Amen!", "Preach!", or "Did say it" meaning,

"Yes, the Word did say that") These are appro-

priate in settings that welcome verbal affirma-

tion of the Word.

3.) Verbal affirmation by the corporate Body (This

is particularly the case when the speaker

asks the audience to repeat, in unison, a phrase

of affirmation such as "This is my Bible; It is

God's Word; I can be what it says I can be; I

can do what it says I can do..."

4,) Non verbal affirmation by individuals *(Head nods, clapping, smiling, eye contact etc...)*

5.) Non verbal affirmation by the corporate Body *(This is particularly demonstrated when the speaker asks the audience to repeat an action such as, "Shake hands with your n e i g h b o r and welcome them into the House of the Lord with an embrace".)*

6.) Silence (Often considered a non verbal indicator, can also be indicative of respect and attentiveness and thus an act of confirmation of the Word

7.) Complimenting Remarks which affirm and confirm the Word

8.) Expressions of uniformity such as dressing in unison on special occasions

9.) Use of technology such as projectors, Sermons placed on Websites, YouTube etc...

10.) Referencing the Word in Individual and Corporate Prayer (*It is so vitally important to pray the current Word that the Lord gives to the Church. For instance, if the Lord sends a Word about deliverance and healing, let the prayer leaders lead the congregation in exercising their faith and praying for deliverance and healing in response to that Word. Even though it is our privilege to pray personal petitions before God, we must be careful not to insensitively change the subject before the congregation has adequate time to respond to the current Word.*

Disconfirmation Principles

The Word of God teaches us to refrain from coarse joking, idle chatter and vain babblings. At first, the Believer might be tempted to think, "I don't have that problem." "I am a fairly orderly person. But if we are honest with ourselves, we can surely think of at least one time when we have spoken idly or in a way that was crude or coarse. What follows is a list of the ways in which we can knowingly or unknowingly disconfirm life-giving messages.

1.) Counter speaking by suggesting an alternative subject to the subject at hand.

2.) Cynical speaking

3.) Insulting

4.) Negative projections of the future

5.) Inappropriate and insensitive joking *(This includes inappropriate remarks about gender, race and physical appearance)*

6.) Speaking defeat or loss in the face of challenge

7.) Sowing a seed of doubt by "suggesting" or inculcating that the leader of the organization, ministry, project etc... is somehow less capable than you or someone else. In Kingdom life, order and respect for authority cannot be dismissed because of talent or ability.

8.) Speaking, rather in jest or seriously, in a negative way about your role and calling in the Body.

Words and Leadership

What we say about a person in leadership can have profound and far-reaching consequences. We as Christians must be very careful about what we say about persons in authority. We can easily sow a seed of doubt (which may or may not be grounded in reality) and cause much harm by violating a code of respect and planting even a small seed of doubt or discord in the minds of those who are following the set leader. Speaking life means we take every opportunity to build and to move the agenda of the moment forward. Such spoken forms of negativity such as innuendo, rumor, liable, slander are what the Bible calls murder and are in total antithesis to what the Lord intended for us to yield with our speech. In fact the Biblical notion of "murder" means character assassination, defamation of reputation or the damaging of one's trustworthiness by implanting cause for suspicion (real or imagined) about a person in the minds of others. And, when we implant these negative thoughts in the minds of people who are associated with the leader we cause considerably more damage and potentially breach the bond of trust among the members of that body.

Some engage in dropping remarks that are
loaded with toxic material that can continue to
cause harm long after the remark was made. God
desires that we handle our thoughts about our
leaders in a way that will promote the Glory of
God and push forward the plan and purpose of
God for that congregation or ministry or group of
believers. It might be a prayer group, an informal
group of friends who meet for a Bible Study on
a regular basis or a Sunday School class. Or as
stated early on, the group might be a congregation. In all of these cases, a leader's role is intri-
cately connected to the success of the group and
the experience of each member of the group. It
is the work of the Holy Spirit to cause all members to bond together and work in synchrony. It
is the responsibility of each member of the group
to pray for one another and to pray especially

for the leader. It is not your responsibility or my responsibility to sway the direction of the group away from the leader if we happen to disagree with him/her. We do not ever want to impart our upset or disagreement with the leader to the larger group. The Word of God says, *six things the Lord hates, yes seven are an abomination to Him (Proverbs 6: 16-19).* One of these is *"sowing discord among brothers"*. We as the Body of Christ are brothers and sisters. We cannot afford to mutilate one another with our words. We cannot afford to oppose the leader of a group by speaking against him/her both verbally and non verbally. Let us make a fresh commitment to honor one another and our leaders with our words of support, encouragement and prayers.

How To Speak Life When Confronting

Say very little...PRAY a whole lot! In the Words of the Psalmist, "Be slow to speak, quick to listen and slow to anger. We are instructed by the Scriptures to remove selfish motivation out of the confrontation. Responding through our emotions and speaking out too fast, we are more likely to say too much or say things we might regret later. When we speak before we have prayed, stepped back and processed the situation, we are also more likely to escalate in our emotional energy. Anger, as stated in the Scriptures, represents the culmination of progressive build-up of disaffection, Emotions and visceral experiences such as jealousy, fury, offense, hurt, disappointment, let-down, betrayal are implied. We are instructed how to prepare comprehensively to deal with our emotions and consequently be in a better place to speak when emotionally effected.

So, you might ask, how do I confront a brother or sister when I feel he/she is involved in some things which are offensive, disagreeable or even sinful? What can I say? Should I say anything? And, should I bring witnesses? Should I expect that I will not ever again be a trusted participant of the group. There are no short cuts to Godly, caring, effective confrontation. How we confront is revealing of what things we value and how we prioritize the things we value. I want to address the specific question about confronting a fellow believer, but first let's explore the sometimes complex relationship between motive and confrontation.

There are several different types of confrontation. For the purposes of this conversation, I would like to focus on two types of confrontation...

Effective and Ineffective. Both involve a decision on the part of the confronter to express his/her affect based upon an unmet need. The unmet need fuels the emotion (anger) and the emotion gives way to words spoken, all in the effort to meet a need. Even though, the speaker is confronting someone that he believes to be acting offensively, he first needs to understand why he feels offended and the effect of the offense on his own heart. The reason why he feels offended and the effect of the offense combine to create or reveal an unmet need in his heart. The person who committed the offense disappointed the confronter's expectations. Those expectations are grounded in a need to see certain behaviors, standards or actions upheld. The offense stems from the fact that the offender violated or failed to uphold these expectations. The confronter must allow the Holy Spirit to deal with his heart first before going to confront or the presence of unmet needs could potentially distort his approach or cloud his purpose.

When dealt with through prayer, unmet needs can work for the good. For instance, I can recall feeling quite angry and "let-down" about one of our son's grades for a particular semester. All of our sons love sports and we have allowed them to play on the condition that they keep their grades up. In this instance, this son had allowed his grades to drop and when confronted he seemed just a little too casual and dismissive. I stepped away from the discussion and confronted him the next day after I had a chance to pray and ask God to filter through my own needs and expectations to see him excel.

This allowed me to speak to him differently. First, I confronted him because he had not kept his commitment to put academics first and sports second. Second, I wanted him to recognize that he had performed lower than his ability. His father and I wanted him to know that it was a parental expectation that he do his absolute best. We wanted him to know that this was non-negotiable, not to fulfill my expectation so that I would feel better about my parenting, no! But this was for his good. We genuinely care about him. We thank God that he responded by doing very well the next semester. Our confrontation was purified by God's grace and then God was able to use our confrontation to call him to a level of performance that he might not have achieved if his poor academic behavior was left unaddressed. So, my unmet need, my expectation that he excel academically first and play sports second was acknowledged in prayer. The emotions, my feelings of let-down and frustration etc...were acknowledged and given over to the Lord in prayer. And, then, the Lord was able to use me to truly confront him. The confrontation at that point was for his good and not for my own selfish ambition or pride.

Sometimes, we experience very powerful emotions that are attached to our expectations of others. I can even become invested in my own expectation of how I believe others should respond or act. In other words, using my son's case as an example, my sense of mothering was linked to my expectation of my son's behavior and when he acted accordingly, I was validated. When he failed to live up to my expectation of him, I was tempted to doubt my ability or success as a mother. Sometimes, we can love so deeply or give so much of ourselves to others that we unconsciously "expect" reciprocal responses from those in whom we have invested so much. The expectation becomes a need. The person's adverse behavior, (they acted in a way that was opposite to your expectation) creates an unmet need.

I don't think God wants us to deny this normal process. I believe we should admit our humanity. For example, the Word of God says that we may become angry, but we are to "sin not". It is our response to these needs that makes the difference. This is why the Scripture explains the storage place of our hearts as "abundance"; "out of the abundance of the heart, the mouth speaks".

Often the presence of conflict is used by the Lord to strengthen us. Even more, the presence of offense can be an opportunity to look inside our own hearts and allow the Holy Spirit to heal us of some hidden or unexpressed longing or need. Most importantly, when we look to the Lord to meet our needs (all of our needs), He will most assuredly meet us at our point of need! Sometimes, He sends the answer through other people. Sometimes we receive what we need directly from the Scriptures. Often, we are the recipients of the Grace of His Presence. This is why it is so vital to spend quality time alone with the Lord.

To summarize, let me return to the original question of confronting a fellow believer. If we follow the general steps outlined above we will bring our hearts before the Lord and ask for His cleansing and His Grace. We will allow Him to purify our motives to make sure that our desire to confront is driven by pure love for the other person and not wounded emotions and unmet needs. I have stated earlier how the Word of God says we are to go to our brother if we are offended or have reason to believe we have offended the person.

Let your attitude be that of a humble servant, not as one who is poised to conquer. Be willing to use words that reveal the problem but restore the person. If the brother is rebellious or disrespectful, we must be firm with him. The Bible says that we must

The Lord teaches us that it is better for a rebel to suffer loss of life but repent and save his soul. Let us make a fresh commitment to repent of pride. Don't be given to quarrels and "endless" debates. Don't allow the enemy to bait us into fruitless discussions that tempt us to compete, covet or castigate one another.

The First Step To Effective Confrontation is Prayer

Effective confrontation begins long before the confrontation when an individual first confronts his/her own need. Ultimately, our needs are addressed spiritually. Accepting the fact that we have needs for significance, acceptance or acknowledgement is an admission to our own vulnerability. This is an act of humility and I have not ever known this process to take place apart from prayer. When we pray, we humble ourselves at the feet of the Father and admit our limitations. We acknowledge that "I am weak (needy) but You, O Lord are strong (All-wise, All-Knowing and Totally Capable of Meeting all of my needs)). This is the most important, first step of confrontation. We must prioritize God's place in our lives, well above the temptation to "set the record straight" or "give him a piece of my mind" or "put her in her place". No. The first, most important step is to recognize that I am in a situation that requires God's Help. Affects were never meant to be handled apart from God. And, the human heart is not designed to respond apart from God's divine guidance through the Holy Spirit.

The Second Step To Effective Confrontation is to Pause

As stated earlier, I have had the opportunity of teaching speech communication for many years. I have taught my students some small steps to diffusing the anxiety that sometimes accompanies public speaking. No step is more simple than the "Pause for a Cause". In other words, when in doubt or fear, uncertainty or over anxious,

PAUSE. Take a deep breath and re-group. This same, simple principle applies to us when preparing to confront.

The Third Step To Effective Confrontation is to Plan

One step that is helpful in the confrontation process is to plan what might be said and what things are not necessary to say. Leave room for flexibility but having a sense of the core issues can help maintain purpose and focus.

The Fourth Step To Effective Confrontation is to Present Your Concern As Clearly As Possible

Clarity is for the speaker, the same as window cleaner is for clouded windows. Clear, concise, well-organized statements take time and effort but the end result is understanding.

Clarity is the result of what I have come to call a clear-minded lifestyle. Let me give you an example from my own life. After a season of prayer, the Holy Spirit revealed to me how I needed to prioritize what I really value so that those valued actions get accomplished first - during the early part of my day while I have peak strength. Even if my day gets hectic, I know I have laid the proper foundation by prioritizing the things that are important and accomplishing them first. As a result of this kind of clear-mindedness, it was easy for me to hear the Lord speaking to me about other areas of my life which are not yet in tact, Clarity produces more clarity which leads to understanding. And, after all, the goal of confrontation is to produce understanding and reconciliation.

Effective confrontation will accomplish several goals. The first is to communicate a concern or affect in a caring way, avoiding hostility, personal vendetta and character defamation. Assure the person of your love and affirmation. After sharing your concern (remember, clarity is key), invite the person to respond. If the response is favorable, you have won your brother/sister. If the response is hostile or defensive, prayerfully wait before proceeding with further explanation of your concern. The person and/or the situation may need more time. Keep in mind that the Holy Spirit is always at work, pruning and sharpening all of us and bringing us more and more into the image of Christ.

The Fifth Step To Effective Confrontation is to Select God's Timing and Place When Confronting

We can trust the Lord to fight our battles for us and to give us wisdom when to speak and when not to speak. Certainly, we do not need to be afraid to speak or shy away from confronting a brother or sister who is living compromisingly. Some practical suggestions include the following:

*Select a time that will not compete for your brother/sister's attention. For instance, if he looks forward to watching football games, then the night of the Super Bowl might not be the best time to plan to talk.

*Select a place that will give you the amount of privacy that you think is necessary for the discussion but also a place that is publicly accessible. For instance, it is not recommended that a single young lady would invite a male adult to her apartment for the purpose of confronting him. An office setting, a restaurant or coffee cafe, a Church meeting room, these are public places that are still conducive to private discussion.

*If possible, when you first introduce the matter, talk with the individual (as the Word of God suggests) alone and assure him/her that you would like to settle the matter privately

*Take a trusted, prayerful person with you if the matter is ultra-sensitive; if there is threat of verbal or emotional violence; if there has been an earlier attempt to confront and the person resisted. (If there is the possibility of physical violence, you will need to prayerfully consider engaging the services of trained security or police officers. For example, a young male student became aggressive towards me when I refused

to change his grade to a higher grade. He was quite physically tall and strong and he lunged at me, raising his hand as if was going to strike me. Thank God he did not hit me and he grabbed his coat and books and left the room. But for the next class, I invited the presence of campus security to enter the room with me. He did not attend the next class and did not stay in the course but it was a challenging experience and it taught me the importance of not trying to take care of things all on my own.)

We can confront in Christ. We can live together in sincere, transparent relationship. Through the power of the Holy Spirit, we are able to prayerfully speak life to our brother/sister and care for them by sharing the truth.

Chapter Six

Acknowledging and Honoring: Speaking and Respecting Authority

"I give honor to all of the Pastors and their wives, Elders, Deacons, Members and Friends...". This is a common opening statement for many preachers/speakers in some traditional African American Churches. This is a context where protocol is intentional and functions like a calling card for the speaker. For example, culturally speaking, some African American Christians identify readily with a speaker who takes the time to give a statement of honor to the Sr. Leaders of the congregation. Such a greeting functions as a confirmation of respect and order. But Churches vary in their faith expressions. One area that is an indication of Church formality is the use of titles - for the Sr. Pastor(s) and with the Pastoral and Lay Leadership. In some Churches, the Pastor is referred to by first name. An example is Pastor Chuck Swindoll. On his daily radio broadcast, his announcer speaks, "Now here's Chuck with some more information about today's message, titled...". There is no disrespect here. Chuck Swindoll is a respected Evangelical leader, nationally and internationally known. Because he is known as Chuck Swindoll in his own cultural circle, he is called the same by people from other cultural traditions. By contrast, I don't think any facilitator would introduce Bishop T.D. Jakes by stating,

"Let's receive our speaker today, T.D...". It is partly because he is known as Bishop T.D. Jakes in his own cultural context and it is expected that people from other cultural traditions would introduce him by using the same title. To use his first name, in a formal setting, could be perceived (not necessarily by him) as disrespect.

In these traditions, the Pastor is given his full title, on every encounter, in every situation. In my own past experience, I recall how this played out even at our annual Church picnics. For the purposes of this discussion, I will call my former Pastor, Bill Brown. We would refer to our Pastor as Pastor Brown, never Bill! Even though we might be saying, "Pastor Brown, please pass the ketchup." We would never, NEVER say, "Bill, please pass the ketchup." Even though the traditions may vary, the spirit of respect and acknowledgement can remain the same. Whether in a formal or informal setting or with people who regard the use of formal protocol or informal familiarity, it is important that we be intentional in regarding one another and regarding the anointing and calling that God has placed on our lives.

In this regard, speaking life is largely a purposeful nod or affirmation, not a preoccupation of titles or fixation on positions. The Word of God teaches us that the man of God who works well is worthy of double honor. This kind of honor is an acknowledgement but not an idolatrous exaltation of any person or position.

The Relationship Between Speaking Life And Submitting To Authority

How can I "speak life" when someone else is "calling the shots"? In God's taxonomy, the powerful often appear as the powerless when in actuality, God empowers those who obey and serve Him. Let's look closer at this Scripture: "...God resists the proud, but gives grace to the humble" (I Peter 5:5). So, what is the link between submission and speaking life? All too often, speaking is seen as evidence of power. To be able to speak, to say whatever is on one's mind is a virtue that is highly esteemed in this culture. Rightfully, we should appreciate our "right to speak". It is a quintessential freedom hard-fought and protected by hundreds and thousands of soldiers and military personnel. Many have given their lives to protect our freedom. But there is another principle that governs this principle. As Christians, we answer to a Divine mandate. It must be that our individual freedoms operate within the context of obedience to God. *Ultimately, the principle of humility governs our individual freedoms.* This means that although we do possess inalienable rights, we voluntarily, willingly and willfully place our rights in submission to the Holy Spirit. Exercising our rights and showcasing our right to exercise our rights becomes a fundamental non-issue inasmuch as pleasing the Father becomes the main goal. So, to speak or not to speak is transferred from the arena of personal expression for expression's sake to obedience to our Heavenly Father and when we obey Him - we are worshipping Him.

When we worship the Lord, we invite His Presence, His Blessing - The Blessing of Life and Liveliness. Whenever Jesus enters a gathering, a situation, a circle of worshippers, His Presence brings life. He Alone, knows what it takes to infuse the atmosphere with life, to turn a situation around and move the direction from a anticipated death to certain life. There's a word my children used in the past when they were expressing surprise or awe at a circumstance or outcome that surpassed their expectation. They would say, "Oh, Snap!" Secretly, I really admire this term and they way they said it. (That cannot be said for all of their slang terms). I know that the use of this term is dated and not as popular perhaps now as it was in the recent past, but this term really captures how I feel, when God does the extraordinary - when He overturns a decision; heals a broken marriage; gives health back to a dying patient; causes the supernatural cancellation of crippling debt...when the world slams a door, locks it, throws the key into the ocean and gives a "final" sentence and then God intervenes! Can't you hear it..."Oh, Snap!" God creates a turn-around, sends the angel to the bottom of the ocean floor, locates that key, unlocks that door and opens it for you! And you walk out free - with a second chance! That's an "Oh, Snap!" moment!!!!

There are two points to remember. First, God knows what it takes for us to receive from Him, what He has for us. It might be a situation when we have the "freedom" to speak, but instead what might be required of you at that moment is submission. The Word of God says, "He has shown you O Man, what is good; and what does the Lord require of you... to walk humbly with your God..." (Micah 6:8). If we speak when we should not speak, we are speaking with the wrong motive. This will not work the purpose of God. If we speak, to prove that we know how to speak; that we are in command of the language and in command of our faculties- the end result will be just that - proof that we can speak. This will never work the purposes of God. In fact, in many cases, we might even cause trouble or make the situation worse because acting in our own flesh, never invites the blessing of the Lord.

Second, submission becomes a type of speaking. As an act of worship, when we submit we are "saying" what God wants us to say to our brother or sister - that we love them and we are willing to allow the Holy Spirit to lead in our dealings with one another. When we do this we are allowing our actions to speak and when we speak in this way, we speak life. In the Communications field, we routinely, watch hours of recorded speakers giving eloquent speeches and fabulous public presentations and we log many more hours studying the origins of words. But even with all of the years of involvement in communication, I can tell you no one, absolutely no one comes even close to teaching us about communication as our Lord, Jesus Christ. He taught us more than the mechanics of speech. Jesus taught us <u>what</u> we should say and <u>why</u> we should speak and <u>how</u> we should speak. He also taught us how to speak without using words, that we can speak through our character and commitment to Him. In essence, Jesus taught us that speaking without purpose is futile and empty, like a person who attempts to swim in a lake without water. The thing that transforms our words, our actions and decisions is the purpose of exalting and lifting up Christ. If it is our endeavor to exalt Him, He will bless our efforts. Sometimes, our efforts might be misunderstood by individuals. For instance, there have been times when I was ridiculed for remaining silent when others expected me to "fight back" with my words. I know I might have appeared docile, weak or unknowledgeable because people expected me to "stand up for yourself" and "give them a piece of your mind" and "let them know that you are not a pushover". But as I followed the leading of the Holy Spirit and waited for His Guidance before speaking, or obeyed Him and did not speak at all, I realized the blessing of doing it God's way and later reaped a greater (much greater!) reward for this obedience. Glory to God for how He leads us and how He protects us even from our own survival instincts and plans to defend ourselves. His purposes are pure and clean and without compromise and He will defend us. Without question, God will fight our battles. But we must cooperate with His Holy Spirit and agrec with Him. What follows is further discussion about the role of agreement in shaping the interplay between submission and authority.

To Speak Or Not To Speak - More About Submission and Authority

When Jesus was confronted with the rejection and disaffection of some of the people of His day, He clarified to them and for us Who He was and is and that He has absolute authority. He states in St. John 10:17 -18 **"Therefore my Father loves Me because I lay down my life that I may take it again. No one takes it from Me but I lay it down of myself. I have power to lay it down**

and I have power to take it again. This command I have received from My Father".

There are several factors at work in this passage. This Scripture helps us to understand that there is submission to authority and submission which is ultimately an expression of authority (in this case Jesus' authority). Jesus, although fully man and fully God, submitted Himself to God, the Father. This submission did not weaken His authority or compromise His power. Rather, Jesus submitted out of His love for His Heavenly Father and His Oneness with the Father's heart.

Let's look closer at the word 'submission'. The prefix 'sub' means under. The central term 'mission' is a derivative of the latin root, mittere which means to cause to go. This gives rise to the latin term 'missio' which means to send. To be on a mission is to be purposefully sent to accomplish,

most generally speaking, the assignment given by
the one (or One) who sent you. Consequently, it
is appropriate and laudable for the person who is
sent to be under the direction of the person who
did the sending; the person who caused him/her
to go. For the believer, submission is yielding to
the Sender for the sake of the mission. It means
placing one's personal inclinations under the
authority of the Lord, the One who sends me on
assignment. It is not necessary for me to understand the assignment or know the outcome
ahead of time, or to be able to predict my challenges. I simply must be willing to come under
His authority.

Because God works through people, His
authority is vested in people. For example, clergy,
deacons, lay leaders and counselors all represent examples of persons of authority in the

local Church. Husbands are granted the headship of the home which means God expects them to lead their families into spiritual maturity and develop their families by providing for them and caring for their needs. So that this mission can be accomplished God has instructed that submission function at four important levels in the home. First, the husband and wife are to submit to God and follow the Lordship of Jesus Christ. Second the husband and wife are to submit to one another in Christian love. Third, the wife is to submit to the husband as unto the Lord and fourth the children are to submit to their parents. These four tiers of submission work like spokes in a tire. It is not a contradictory parallel but rather an alignment fashioned by God designed to purge the family of attitudes and character flaws which are detrimental to the existence and effectiveness of the family if left unaddressed. It is also designed by God to lead the family to success and fulfillment. For instance, consider what happens when the children are leading the parents and not vice versa. Perhaps, it might be in the area of food choices or bed times or playmates. What would happen if the child determines the daily dinner menu. Pizza, cheeseburgers, hot dogs and soda might be alright as occasional foods but if this becomes the steady diet, surely there will be some health problems as a result. No milk! No veggies (there is no substitute for collard greens)! No or very little whole grains! It is the parent who understands the value of nutritious meals and therefore the parent's responsibility to provide leadership in determining the daily diet.

Our attitude toward persons of authority ought to be one of respect and supportiveness when appropriate. We show this largely by how we respond with our words and our nonverbal behavior. Most of the time this is difficult because we are tempted to think our own sense of authority is equal to their authority. After all, I'm a human being just like he is a human being. This is true, but not the only truth about authority. Equality can co-exist with authority. We can be equals with a person and still be submitted to him or her because of his position and place of authority. Equality refers to essential identity while authority refers to essential identity and assignment or role. For example, much of my authority in our home rests on the fact that I am a wife to my husband. But at the same time, any authority that I might have is ultimately grounded in Christ. In line with what Jesus declared, "Therefore My Father loves Me", therefore, whether you love me or not, <u>My</u>

<u>Father loves Me.</u> Having the love of the Heavenly Father is what really matters. We can make Jesus' declaration our own. "My Father loves me". I know to Whom I really report and answer to. He is the Living God and He makes all final decisions. Another example comes to mind. There are times when I am wrangling with a purchase order via the telephone. Perhaps, I feel I am not getting what I need from the attendant so I will say, Please let me speak to your supervisor or manager...why? Because I know that the supervisor is the one who makes the final decisions. He/she is the person who will make a difference in my case. In similar ways, when we are called upon to submit our natural tendency to explain, lead or execute plans to the leadership and authority that God has placed over us, we should quickly

recognize that God is the One who has the final say. The Lord is always the One who is in control.

Often, God will arrange circumstances so that we will be able to express our insights and positions with the blessing of better timing, better receptivity and without compromise. The most important factor is that we are flowing in obedience to the Holy Spirit and allowing the Fruit of the Spirit - righteousness, self-control, peace... to develop and grow in our character and this is pleasing to the Lord. After all, the higher purpose is to please and honor the Lord.

THOUGHT CHECK

Recall a time when you felt betrayed, wrongly accused or misunderstood. Describe your emotions - were you angry? Describe your thoughts. Now try to remember what did you say? Did you use words that you wished you had not used? How would you want to respond the next time you are in a similar situation?

Prayer Focus....Take a moment to pray and ask the Lord to cleanse you from speaking out of an angry heart. Invite the Holy Sprit to fill you and produce the fruit of righteousness in you; to sanctify your emotions and thereby cause you to speak life

Chapter Seven

Sowing and Increasing - Speaking Prosperity

Blessed are you who sow beside all waters

(Isaiah 32:20)

I remember one of the favorite sayings of my Dad and I remember exactly how he would say it. He would gently twirl on his neatly trimmed moustache, shake his head a few times and fully extend his free hand upward, making the sign for the number two, " Two plus two <u>always</u> equals four". He might continue with the expression, "something doesn't add up". This meant that the information he was analyzing was woefully deficient in the logic area. In other words there was a break down in the logical coherence of the story or accounting etc... In the natural sense, whatever we sow, we will reap. This is a basic law of nature. If we sow carrot seeds, we will harvest carrots, tomato seeds means harvesting tomatoes etc...

This is also true in the spiritual sense. However, the spiritual sowing and reaping can in some ways be described as sowing and increasing. It is true that you will reap what you sow, but a very important spiritual dynamic exploits this truth. Now only will you reap what you sow, but your harvest will increase exponentially, compared to what you've sown. If we sow 2 seeds, we will harvest far more than two pieces of fruit. If we sow or give an hour of time, we get back far more in return in our work, service or relationships. That is why this chapter is called sowing and increasing. Let me say again that this is not intended to manipulate the truth of God's Word that says we shall reap what we sow. This teaching is fundamental to the Christian faith and reveals much about character development and responsibility. If we are kind and thoughtful, kindness and thoughtfulness is multiplied back to us. If we are merciful, the Word of God says that to the merciful, He will show mercy.

We can see passage after passage that explains the principle of reciprocity. If you dish it out, you will receive it back in like measure. This is a law of nature and spirit, however God is never confined to a single box - an insular principle. Like a balloon which can inflate and soar, sowing takes on another dimension in light of the following truths:

*There must be sowing before there can be reaping

*Sowing must always precede the reaping

*The reaping will always yield far more than that which was sown

*Consequently, sowing increases the ability of the sower to sow (Another way of saying that - sowing is a means by which the sower increases which then enables him/her to sow more...and increase more...and consequently have more to sow...and increase more...and sow more...and on and on!)

Fundamentally, spiritual sowing is done in terms of giving. We tithe, give offerings, time, volunteer our services, abilities and give of ourselves in many ways. The Word of God says we even sow in tears. There is yet another type of sowing I believe we do not consider very much. That is the sowing that is done with our mouths. Yes, we sow in words. Here is the exciting news about sowing in words! If we sow in words, we will reap words, but not only words. Words sown in the spiritual sense can reap and manifest in the physical. This is not a magical, whimsical observation, no, but rather a spiritual principle.

Let's look closer. There are several Scriptures which express the potential of words to create and change people and situations. For example, I will point to two Scriptures here, "The power of life and death are in the tongue" and "And they overcame him by the Blood of the Lamb and the word of their testimony." (Rev 12:11)

For this discussion, let us consider the speaking of words as a type of sowing. This kind of sowing takes two basic directions. The first direction is unilateral; that is speaking or sowing words of blessing into the lives of other people. This is directly speaking life into another person. For instance, I can remember when our children were younger and were afraid to go to sleep in the dark at nighttime. Their father and I would speak to them and assure them that Jesus was with them and that they were safe and secure in Jesus for the whole night. We would augment this assurance by refraining from watching television an hour or two before their bedtime, replacing stressful music with peaceful music and generally speaking in ways that would de-stress the environment. Soon, our sons became "happy sleepers". As they grew older they seemed to sleep well and generally enjoy the notion of "stretching out in their own beds" or "hitting the sack".

Anything that threatens our peace of mind or diminishes our quality of life in Christ becomes a life snatcher, taking away from us and hindering our growth and progress. Words spoken in good faith can reverse that downward curse and restore, give balance, give hope or renew. Speaking such words constitute speaking life. This kind of speaking creates an atmosphere for improvement and goes a long way to point people in right directions in their lives. But unilateral speaking alone cannot do what is ultimately needed in order for people to be set free. This brings us to the second type of speaking (sowing). This is speaking the Word of God both to people and by the power of the Holy Spirit.

We've talked about speaking life in various contexts, speaking in authority, in submission to authority, speaking in victory and more. This chapter reminds us that we have God's permission to speak to our finances, speak to our vocational fields, our businesses, our produce and productivity and command these areas of our lives to prosper. Prosperity is defined as the simple consistency of progress and balance of well-being in every area of our lives. This teaching does not negate the role, purpose and benefits of suffering and Christian empathy. The struggle for justice and equality, for instance, was a necessary response to the evil of oppression levied against people of Color in this country decades ago (and still exists in some contexts), but our God is the God of triumph and overcoming power. He invites His people to trust and believe Him for progress and advancement. God does not desire to prosper us for our own selfish gain but rather for us to be stronger, more responsible and more able stewards of the heavenly charge - to know Christ and make Him known.

We should strongly and firmly make our speech reflect the spiritual reality that God is our Victory and Triumph and speak the Word of God over our lives and our fields.

Chapter Eight

Blessing...Speaking Life

A wholesome tongue is a tree of life

(Proverbs 15:4)

Aparticularly fond memory is of a visit to a former classmate who lives with her husband in a beautifully restored 200 year old Maine farmhouse. Mae and Mike (Assumed names to preserve their identity) are a loving couple who had obviously poured many hours of painstaking work into their lovely home. Wide clapboard wood floors had been carefully revitalized. The big, inviting kitchen was filled with bright sunlight and well-tended hanging plants. State-of-the-art stainless steel appliances and several loaves of freshly baked bread made this a warm and welcoming environment.

At the end of the evening, Mae showed my husband and me to our guest quarters for the night, an entire suite on the second floor of their home which included a bedroom with an over-stuffed wrought iron queen-sized bed. Our bed was positioned so that we could see outside the open window. With a cool, summer breeze and moonlight spilling into our room, we could see the leafy fullness of a huge oak tree. The branches spanned out over the lawn and the leaves swayed gently in the night air. In the morning, the stately tree seemed even larger. It gave shelter from the sun and provided a home for numerous little animals like squirrels and birds. It was so beautiful... and so alive! As I read Proverbs 15:4, my experience at my friend, Mac's house is what comes to mind. Everything about being with her and her husband was refreshing. It was restful, inviting, clean, calming and uplifting. In that atmosphere, my husband and I relaxed and the four of us laughed, broke bread together. When we left, we felt renewed. Mae and Mike were excellent hosts. And, when I recall the tree outside the guest bedroom window I see it as a metaphor for how God intends our words to function.

When we speak, we should be excellent hosts with our words. Our words should create shade for people when there is a need to cover or help them recover from harshness and cruelty. Our words should bring increase and foster productivity. Like a canopy of beauty, our words can envelope all who hear us and allow their spirits to soar.

Are your words a fresh breeze? A gentle wave? Soothing? Are your words clean and inviting? Do your words bring life? There is ultimately one way to ensure that we are speaking blessing and that is to align our speaking with the Word of God. Allowing the Holy Spirit to breathe fresh life into our hearts daily by the renewing of our minds through the reading of the Word of God, this is what will transform the way we talk. As the Lord enlivens us, we become streams of blessings to others. Yes, a wholesome tongue is a tree of life. The Lord invites us to share the blessing with others. He invites us to speak life.

Words Like Life

Words Like *Fresh*

cool breeze, the leafy green

Bringing forth, in its season

By the river, Planted.

The yielding fruit of sweet

Of Dew And Morning

Like *fresh*

Words, like *seed*

Sown into open hearts

Words of love, words of power

Words of strength

Words Like *seed*

Speaking, Blessing...Giving Life

Words

Words like *life*

Notes

1. Proverbs 10:11

2. Proverbs 10:13

3. St. John 17:13, 21, 22

4. II Corinthians 5:18

5. James 3:5

6. James 3:4

7. James 3:8

8. James 3:10

9. Romans 7

10. Esther 4:13-14

11. Esther 2:17

12. Ephesians 5:12

13. Ephesians 5:8

14. Hebrews 12:25

15. Psalm 40:10

16. Romans 10:17

17. Psalm 118:24

18. Romans 10:14-15

19. Exodus 20:8-10

20. Hebrews 10:24-25

21. Genesis 1:2

22. Ephesians 4:11-15

23. Joshua 1:1-8

24. Joshua 1:10-16

25. Hebrews 11:6

26. I John 5:4

27. Rev 12

28. Proverbs 6:16-19

29. Micah 6:8

30. I Peter 5:5

31. St. John 10:17-18

32. Isaiah 32:20

References

Armstrong, Richard. *The Pastor-Evangelist in Worship.* (1986) The Westminster Press. Philadelphia, PA.

Asare, Seth. *Interview on Impartation.* (February, 2011) Boston College, Mass

Edwards, Troy, *Interview on Impartation.* *(February, 2011)* Warwick, Rhode Island

Greenleaf Robert. *The Power Of Servant Leadership*. (1998) Barrett-Koehler Publishers, San Francisco.

Hackman, Michael, Johnson, Craig. *Leadership A Communication Perspective*. (2000) Waveland Press, Prospect Heights, Illinois

Quainoo, Joseph. *Interview on Impartation*. (January 2010). Providence, Rhode Island

Robinson, Haddon. Biblical Preaching The Development and Delivery Of Expository Messages. (2005) Baker Academic, Grand Rapids, Michigan.

West, Richard, Turner, Lynn. *Introducing Communication Theory.* (2010) McGraw & Hill. N.Y.

Wilson, Fredericka. *Interview on Impartation (February, 2011)* Indianapolis, Indiana

All inquiries may be sent to:

Vquainoo@mail.uri.edu

CPSIA information can be obtained at www.ICGtesting.com
264473BV00003B/3/P